FEMINIST FAMILY THERAPY

Edited by Kathleen M. May

THE FAMILY PSYCHOLOGY AND COUNSELING SERIES

Developed Collaboratively by the American Counseling Association and
the International Association of Marriage and Family Counselors

FEMINIST FAMILY THERAPY

10 9 8 7 6 5 4 3 2 1

American Counseling Association
5999 Stevenson Avenue
Alexandria, VA 22304

Director of Publications
Carolyn C. Baker

Copy Editor
Elaine Dunn

Cover design by Martha Woolsey

Library of Congress Cataloging-in-Publication Data

Feminist family therapy / edited by Kathleen M. May
   p. cm. (The family psychology and counseling series)
   Includes bibliographical references.
   ISBN 1-55620-207-5 (alk. paper)
   1. Family psychotherapy. 2. Feminist therapy. I. May, Kathleen M., 1944-
RC488.5.F4448 2000
616.89'156—dc21   00-035569

The Family Psychology and Counseling Series

In Preparation

High-Performing Families: Causes, Consequences, and Clinical Solutions
Bryan E. Robinson, PhD, and Nancy D. Chase, PhD

Integrative and Biopsychosocial Therapy
Len T. Sperry, MD, PhD

Practical Approaches for School Counselors: Integrating Family Counseling in School Settings
Lynn D. Miller, PhD

Techniques in Marriage and Family Counseling, Volume Two
Richard E. Watts, PhD

Advisory Board

■■■

THE FAMILY PSYCHOLOGY AND COUNSELING SERIES

Table of Contents

From the Series Editor

Language inevitably structures one's own
experience of reality, as well as the experience
of those to whom one communicates.
—*Rachel Hare-Mustin and Jeanne Marecek (1990)*

Girls and women necessarily have different experiences than
do boys and men, and these differential experiences generate
distinctive modes of thinking, judging, relating, and so forth. The
field of counseling and psychotherapy with women is relatively new.
Books on counseling women were not published until the 1970s
(e.g., Chesler, 1972; Chodorow, 1978; Miller, 1976). There are a number
of core issues related to the mental health of women that suggest
the need for a specialty in counseling and therapy with women.
Among these are

1. The special problems that women bring into the therapeutic
   setting.
2. Sexual socialization and the development of women.
3. Inadequacies of contemporary theory, research, and practice
   addressing the lives of women.
4. The development of alternative approaches to conceptualization and intervention with women.

The application of these feminist principles to family counseling and therapy with women requires additional integration of theory with practice.

At the root of feminist family therapy is a commitment to overcome the commonplace stereotypes of gender differences and to eliminate the biases that suppress women and also men in society. As we enter a new millennium, the influence of gender on how we live our lives is still under question. What we have previously accepted as scientific truth about women and men is being challenged by new knowledge, questions, and philosophies. The "automatic" acceptance of self-interest and power as important is being investigated. Theories, therapies, and language that invisibly empower some and oppress others are finally being identified. At the heart of this movement is feminist therapy. This particular monograph looks at how issues of gender affect families and family therapy. This monograph is a compilation of the work of professional counselors who are at the cutting edge of feminist or gender-fair scholarship. Their work not only enlightens the reader but also challenges the very heart of our professional psychological traditions. Kathleen M. May and her colleagues provide both an invitation and a challenge to this important area. If you read this monograph, you will never conduct therapy in the same way.

—Jon Carlson, PsyD, EdD
Series Editor

References

Chesler, P. (1972). *Women and madness*. Garden City, NY: Doubleday.

Chodorow, N. (1978). *The reproduction of mothering: Psychoanalysis and the sociology of gender*. Berkeley: University of California Press.

Hare-Mustin, R., & Marecek, J. (Eds.). (1990). *Making a difference: Psychology and the construction of gender*. New Haven, CT: Yale University Press.

Miller, J. B. (1976). *Toward a new psychology of women*. Boston: Beacon Press.

Preface

Working with couples and families has long been a challenge for therapists. Many of the traditional family therapy approaches are predicated on the myth of the nuclear model family and fail to take into account political and cultural realities. The goal of this monograph is to assist professionals in their understanding of the limits of traditional approaches and the promise of feminist family therapy.

Part I (chapters 1 through 4) provides the groundwork for understanding feminist family therapy and its applicability to all families. May (chapter 1) defines feminist family therapy and articulates its major premises and goals. For some families, gender stereotypes and power inequities limit the possibilities for meaningful and positive relationships. In chapter 2, Arnold addresses the omissions and inadequacies of feminist family therapy for women of color and their families. Arnold describes common themes related to the lives of women of color and illustrates how feminist family therapists can better serve them. Honoring differences and the realities of the lives of women of color is stressed. Seem (chapter 3) demonstrates the pervasiveness of the dominant culture's stereotypes and myths about homosexuality and points out the imperative for feminist family therapists to become aware of their own homophobia and heterosexism. She illustrates some feminist strategies to help same-sex and bisexual couples and families articulate their voices and gain knowledge of themselves. In chapter 4, MohdZain describes how gender socialization and stereotypes harm men. He specifies the benefits of feminist family therapy for men and how such an approach expands men's options to lead more satisfying lives.

Part II (chapters 5 through 9) takes a closer look at feminist family therapy's applicability to families in different stages of the family life cycle and to a variety of presenting concerns. In chapter 5, Sands and Petersen describe the power of a feminist family therapy approach when working with adolescents and their families. Using two case studies from their own practices, they illustrate the application of feminist principles to the problems of drug abuse and ungovernability. Looking at the other end of life's continuum, Staton (chapter 6) brings us a personal account of counseling an elderly woman from a feminist family therapy perspective. She demonstrates how the therapist's own biases and assumptions about families and aging can limit the client's capacity for growth and development. Giordano and Bull-Welsh (chapter 7) describe how feminist family therapy approaches offer insights into the gendered nature of anger and ways in which gender stereotypes affect the expression of anger. Strategies to expose underlying gender dynamics embedded in anger are described and demonstrated through a case study that the authors discussed in supervision. In chapter 8, Hunt and Matthews depict the intersection of feminist family therapy and rehabilitation counseling. They articulate the supporting philosophies of feminist family therapy and rehabilitation. Using a case study, Hunt and Matthews show how feminist family therapy can expand the options for healthy family functioning when a family member has a disability. Finally, in chapter 9, Foster expresses the need to develop a feminist understanding of sexuality. She describes how sexuality, through therapeutic isolation from the total human experience, is objectified and isolated from sociopolitical and cultural realities. In a case study, Foster illustrates strategies for bringing sexuality to the forefront in clinical practice.

Part III consists of an edited transcript of Kathleen M. May's interview with Cheryl Rampage, a leader in the field of feminist family therapy. May and Rampage cover a number of topics regarding feminism and feminist family therapy. Rampage provides a moving account of her own search for understanding gender stereotypes and power imbalances and how to bring such issues into the therapy room.

All of the authors of this monograph offer a perspective that is grounded in an appreciation of cultural context, the effects of gender stereotypes, and the importance of collaborative relationships between families and therapists. It is my hope that this book will increase family counselors' understanding of feminist family therapy and its applicability to all families.

—*Kathleen M. May, PhD*

Biographies

Kathleen M. May, PhD, is an associate professor in the counselor education program at the University of Virginia and coordinator of the master's program in mental health counseling. She teaches courses in couples and family counseling as well as mental health counseling. Dr. May has been a feminist for as long as she can remember and has practiced feminist therapy throughout her career. She is a licensed mental health counselor in Florida, a National Certified Counselor, and a National Board of Certified Counselor-approved clinical supervisor. At present, she enjoys considering the place of feminist theory in counseling, training, and supervision. Dr. May and her partner of 27 years, Frazier Solsberry, have two Labrador retrievers, Muddy Waters and Billie Holiday.

Jon Carlson, PsyD, EdD, is distinguished professor at Governors State University in University Park, Illinois, and director of the Lake Geneva Wellness Clinic in Wisconsin. He is the founding editor of *The Family Journal: Counseling and Therapy for Couples and Families* and has served as president of the International Association of Marriage and Family Counselors. Dr. Carlson holds a diplomate in family psychology from the American Board of Professional Psychology. He is a fellow of the American Psychological Association and a certified sex therapist by the American Association of Sex Educators, Counselors, and Therapists. He has authored over 25 books and 125 professional articles. He has received numerous awards for his professional contributions from major professional organizations, including the American Counseling Association, the Association for Counselor Education and Supervision, and the American Psychological Association. Dr. Carlson and his spouse of 32 years, Laura, are the parents of five children and grandparents of two.

Contributors

Mary Smith Arnold, PhD, is a professor in the Division of Psychology and Counseling at Governors State University, University Park, Illinois.

Sue Bull-Welsh, MsEd, is the coordinator of the Women's Program at Alexian Brothers Northwest Mental Health Center, DeKalb, Illinois.

Victoria A. Foster, PhD, is an associate professor in the School of Psychology and Counselor Education and the director of New Horizons Family Counseling Center at the College of William and Mary, Williamsburg, Virginia.

Francesca G. Giordano, PhD, is an associate professor in the Department of Psychology, Counseling, and Special Education at Northern Illinois University, DeKalb, Illinois.

Brandon Hunt, PhD, is an associate professor in the Department of Counselor Education, Counseling Psychology, and Rehabilitative Services at The Pennsylvania State University, University Park, Pennsylvania.

Connie Matthews, PhD, is an assistant professor in the Department of Counselor Education, Counseling Psychology, and Rehabilitative Services at The Pennsylvania State University, University Park, Pennsylvania.

A. Zaidy MohdZain, PhD, is an assistant professor in Educational Administration and Counseling at Southeast Missouri State University, Cape Girardeau, Missouri.

Suni Petersen, PhD, is an assistant professor in the Department of Counseling Psychology at Temple University, Philadelphia, Pennsylvania.

Tovah Sands, PhD, is an assistant professor in the Department of Educational Psychology and Counseling at California State University, Northridge, California.

Susan R. Seem, PhD, is an associate professor and chair of the Department of Counselor Education at the State University of New York College at Brockport, Brockport, New York.

A. Renee Staton, PhD, is an assistant professor in the Counseling Psychology Program at James Madison University, Harrisonburg, Virginia.

PART

UNDERSTANDING
FEMINIST FAMILY THERAPY:
DIVERSE PERSPECTIVES

Feminist Family Therapy Defined

Kathleen M. May, PhD

Some of my young women graduate students shy away from the term *feminist* because they think "those issues" are history. Before considering the value of a feminist approach to family therapy, they have to be convinced that the term has a contemporary relevance. I tell them: Feminism is about expanding opportunities, possibilities, options, and the acceptable range of feelings for all women and men. It seeks to rectify the inequities in our society that are based on gender.

Feminism

Feminist family therapy has its roots in feminist theory. According to Walters, Carter, Papp, and Silverstein (1988),

> Feminism is a humanistic framework or worldview concerned with roles, rules, and functions that organize our society and male–female interactions. Feminism seeks to include the experiences of women in all formulations of human experience and to eliminate the dominance of male assumptions. (p. 17)

Feminism is more than an impartial stance, more than a gender-fair or nonsexist stance, for these stances ignore women's history

(Russell, 1984). Feminism requires a redistribution of power and responsibility between the sexes. Feminism aims to bring an end to the allocation of roles and functions on the basis of gender and, instead, to allow interests, abilities, and personal choice to determine people's course in life.

Feminist views, like most broad-based philosophical perspectives, are themselves extraordinarily heterogeneous. "Feminist theory is not one, but many, theories or perspectives and each feminist theory or perspective attempts to describe women's oppression, to explain its causes and consequences, and to prescribe strategies for women's liberation" (Tong, 1989, p. 1). Limitations of space force me to sacrifice depth and breadth in terms of articulating the commonalities and differences among the various perspectives such as liberal, Marxist, radical, or existential feminism. This monograph is mainly an introduction to some major themes in feminist thought and feminist family therapy.

Almost all feminists' positions start from the premise that society now and in the past has been arranged hierarchically by gender and that such arrangements must be challenged. Such a position is the one that is stressed in this monograph. The significance of women's experiences of oppression and their perspective of the world is the focus.

Most variations of feminism do not blame individual men for the patriarchal social system that exists; feminism does seek to understand and change the socialization process that keeps men and women thinking and acting within a sexist, male-dominated framework (Walters et al., 1988). Feminists do assert that gender inequities are built into the very fabric and structure of U.S. society and that this imbalance must be changed. This change requires a reduction in power and privilege for men and an increase in power for women. Increased freedom and an increased sense of partnership for women may well affect reduction in power and privilege for men. It is not about women gaining and men losing; it is about equality.

Male–Female Socialization

Many theories and models of healthy functioning are based on male socialization, effectively ignoring the socialization process of women and inappropriately assigning pathology or dysfunction. Male models are considered human models, and women suffer accordingly. Stereotypical male characteristics are valued; female characteristics are devalued (Miller, 1986). These gendered roles affect the ability of the many family units to function effectively and to meet the needs of all members of the family. Both men and women are harmed; the harm to women is greater (Goodrich, Rampage, Ellman, & Halstead, 1988).

Whereas men are socialized within the framework of individual achievement (autonomy, competition, and isolation), women are socialized in their identification with others, relationship to others, and caring for others (connectedness, relatedness, affiliation, and attachment; Gilligan, 1982). Each of these gender-shaped roles is unidimensional, one restricting connectedness to others, the other limiting the experience of self. These roles are not innate but the result of socialization. "Feminine qualities" in and of themselves are not the problem but rather the low value that patriarchy assigns to these qualities.

What needs to be challenged is the idea that a particular sexual division of labor is inevitable and mutually exclusive. The very concept of gender roles exaggerates the differences between men and women. "It is our construction of gender that emphasizes difference, polarity, and hierarchy rather than similarity, equality, and commonality of human thought and actions" (Hare-Mustin, 1989, p. 73). This dichotomized thinking leads to hierarchical thinking in which one polar opposite becomes more valued than the other does. In our patriarchal society, autonomy and masculinity are valued, and relatedness and femininity are devalued.

Feminists promote androgyny in the sense of encouraging men and women to combine "male" and "female" qualities within themselves. Women are challenged to repossess and develop those aspects of themselves that they have previously rejected or ignored because of their masculine connotations; men are challenged to repossess and develop those aspects of themselves that they have previously rejected or ignored because of their feminine connotations (Russell, 1984). Cooperative and flexible relationships in which roles can be equivalent or complementary, with none of the stresses of hierarchical relationships, are advocated.

Feminism and the Family

Throughout history, "family" has been the social institution that has stood at the very center of society. It makes sense that feminists would focus attention on the family. For most people, the family is the most important group to which they belong throughout their lives. It is the primary socializing agent and a continuing force in shaping people's lives. Families are where, through gendered parenting, people *become* their gendered selves (Goldner, 1985).

"Gender and gendering of power are not secondary mediating variables *affecting* family life; they *construct* family life in the deepest sense" (Goldner, 1989, p. 56). The family is also the patriarchal structure that has silenced, oppressed, and exploited women. Feminists are committed to the task of rebalancing and redefining families.

Critical to the understanding of feminist views of the family is their belief that the "traditional" or "normal" family is a myth. The so-called traditional family sets up the "alternative" family that is then viewed as deviant. Any family that does not consist of father, mother, and children is inferior. Feminists reject this stereotypical, inaccurate description of the family on both historical and moral grounds. Historically, it attributes a sense of false generalization to a family type, which is of relatively recent creation and continuously in transformation. This false historical attribution is then used to give legitimacy to one family type and not others (Nicholson, 1997). In fact, the "normal" family prescribes an oppressive role for women—and men (Goodrich et al., 1988).

Origins of Feminist Family Therapy

Feminist therapy and feminist family therapy evolved from the feminist consciousness of those in the field who experienced a discrepancy between their own experiences as women and those described by the theories they were required to learn and apply (Walters et al., 1988). These feminist therapists observed that the oppression of women was as present and as damaging in counseling and therapy as it was in the society at large (Laidlaw & Malmo, 1990). The impact of cultural norms, social expectations, and political structures in the lives of women was virtually ignored. Therapeutic approaches developed by and based on culturally empowered White men were indiscriminately and systemically misapplied to culturally disempowered women (and other disempowered people).

The formation of the Women's Project in Family Therapy in 1977 by Marianne Walters, Peggy Papp, Betty Carter, and Olga Silverstein is often credited with the birth of feminist family therapy. This project was devoted to raising and studying issues related to women in families and in the family therapy field. In June 1978, the first two articles on feminist approaches to family therapy appeared in the professional literature. Hare-Mustin's article, "A Feminist Approach to Family Therapy," was published in *Family Process*, and Hare-Mustin and Hines's article, "Ethical Concerns in Family Therapy," appeared in *Professional Psychology*. These feminist perspectives demonstrated how traditional approaches neglect and distort the experiences of women and contribute to the continual confinement and oppression of women. Traditional, male-based family therapy principles were filtered, feminized, and reinterpreted to fit the experiences of women. Family therapy was enlarged and enriched by defining family systems to include the arena of gender socialization and power and their impact on family life. Main themes that emerged were the integration of reason and emotion, of the personal and the political, and of the relational and the instrumental (Goodrich et al., 1988).

Feminist therapy and feminist family therapy are not additional theories or approaches but rather applications of the feminist perspective to therapeutic work. Feminist therapies offer a point of view about gender hierarchy and other societal constructions and their impact as well as ways to address them in therapy. Feminist family therapy aims at changing the ingrained beliefs that have maintained relationships that are oppressive to women and to men. Feminist family therapists are concerned with division of labor and assignment of roles within the family that are based on stereotypical views of men and women. In general, feminist family therapists recognize and make explicit the destructive and dysfunctional influence of these gendered roles on the expression of women's competence within and outside the family and on men's restrictive emotional expressiveness and nurturing abilities (Feldman, 1982).

Feminist family therapists also recognized the overriding importance of the power structure within the family. Power dynamics within families had not been recognized as such because they were perceived as natural or benign. Feminists documented not only how domestic violence and sexual abuse were connected to differentials of power and dependency of women on men but also the subtler modes of power that operate within families. Examples of these modes of power include spouses' different amount of influence over important family decisions, the unequal division of labor within the family, and the spouses' unequal anticipated costs of living in the relationship. Women lost and men gained. The importance of attending to gender inequality within families was clearly established.

Feminist therapists differ from their nonfeminist colleagues in a number of ways (Laidlaw & Malmo, 1990, pp. 3–5). They understand that women constitute an oppressed group in society and the psychological effects of this oppression on women. They reject the gendered stereotypes of women and men as limiting, distorting, and unhealthy. They recognize the many ways these stereotypes are learned and maintained. They reject an adjustment model of mental health that encourages men and women to conform to societal expectations and norms. Feminist family therapists demystify the therapeutic process and minimize the professional distance and power imbalances between themselves and their clients.

Failure to attend to gender inequality and the differentials of power maintains oppression and supports the traditional sexist arrangements still operating in most families. Feminist family therapists believe therapists have a social responsibility to create a context in which equality of obligations within families might flourish. Feminist family therapists challenge family members not only to develop insights about their roles in maintaining oppressive familial and societal contexts of which they are a part but also to take responsibility for changing them. There is a powerful link between feminism and the genuine valuing of families. Elements of family life that unduly confine and oppress women (and men) must be reformed. Feminist family therapists are concerned with interventions and techniques that maintain the status quo and, therefore, perpetuate people's oppression.

> The way that therapists think of the world is the most power-
> ful factor in family therapy. Despite a therapist's presumed
> neutrality, family therapy is not value-free, whether it involves
> a psychodynamic stance or systems approach. Even neutrality
> itself represents a value. The idea of therapeutic neutrality denies
> the fact that all therapists hold normative concepts of good
> and poor functioning, growth and stagnation, male and female.
> These are so embedded in the therapeutic system, and in fact,
> in Western thinking as to rarely receive comment. (Hare-Mustin,
> 1989, p. 62)

Family Systems Concepts

Feminist family therapists question family therapy's main concepts and how they disadvantage women. They ask whether concepts are explained in the context of unequal distribution of power in the family itself and in the larger social systems. If not, the concept may be oppressive to women and may perpetuate inequality between men and women. For example, the notion of circular causality dominates family systems thinking. This view of causality is nonlinear; rather, family members are involved in recursive patterns of behavior that are reactively instigated and mutually reinforced. One event does not cause another event; both cause each other. The emphasis on circular causality with the exclusion of the acknowledgment of a power differential between men and women has been harmful to women. To adhere to a circular view of causality is, at least in part, to blame the "victim." Circular causality is particularly offensive in situations of domestic violence or abuse. It implies that both partners are engaging in a mutual causal pattern and are equally responsible. Furthermore, circular causality implies that all behavior originates within the interaction itself, which makes it impossible to search for causes outside the interaction, such as cultural beliefs.

Feminist family therapists find other family systems concepts supporting patriarchy and call for reform. Fusion or enmeshment, distance, hierarchy, boundaries, and differentiation are all gendered concepts, formulations that are permeated by male values. These terms and the like almost always refer to specific behaviors being carried out by men or women because of social mandates; they are not neutral terms describing dysfunctional positions (Goodrich et al., 1988; Walters et al., 1988).

The Role of Feminist Family Therapists

Feminist therapists are partners with the families they counsel. The relationship between the therapist and the family is one of collaboration. An authoritative or expert counseling stance found in many traditional family therapy theories is simply not compatible with the egalitarian feminist perspective. Furthermore, feminist family therapists do not believe in a "neutral" or "objective" therapeutic position. In reality, a therapist who assumes a "neutral" stance is supporting traditional sexist arrangements and the prevailing status quo. A neutral stance also keeps men and women prisoners of their genders, reproduces the social pretense that there is equality between men and women, and inadvertently stabilizes an oppressive system. In short, "neutrality means leaving the prevailing patriarchal assumptions implicit, unchallenged, and in place" (Walters et al., 1988, p. 18). Feminist family therapists challenge the notion of neutrality as an appropriate position for a therapist. Neutrality is considered a sham because a neutral stance assumes equal power for each partner in the relationship. Closely connected to the neutral stance are formulations that purport to be gender-free. These formulations are actually sexist because they reproduce the social pretense that there is equality between men and women (Hare-Mustin, 1998).

Skerrett (1996) proposed that mutuality is the centerpiece of feminist practice and further proposed that mutuality become the centerpiece of therapy as well. The process of therapy is viewed largely as an effort to explore and enhance the capacity for relational mutuality. This focus assists men in regaining what has been "lost" and helps validate women in their pursuit of authentic connection. Feminist family therapists also stress the ability to function flexibly, modeling both authoritative and instrumental stances.

Feminist family therapists are consciously and deliberately active in presenting the feminist perspective to the families they counsel. They are clear about communicating counseling goals and their underlying values to families. Foremost, feminist family therapists use a gender lens, and through such a lens, they make explicit issues of power. They help couples examine how their gender beliefs and gender roles constrain them from solving their problems (Rampage, 1998). In therapy, "the feminist theme opens up the picture, the story, the dialogue so that more is seen—the political, social, economic, and cultural context in which differences emerge or get construed" (Parker, 1998, p. 21). "It is the responsibility of the therapist to address gender issues and make them explicit to the family precisely because the family cannot see its problems as gender related" (Goodrich et al., 1988, p. 21).

Feminists believe that, for many families and couples who present themselves for therapy, problems can be traced back to inequalities in power and gender socialization. According to Sims (1996), these inequalities in power are the product of the uneven skills of the partners to say what they know and to hear the other with respect. These differences in skills are the product of gendered socialization and patriarchy. Goals of therapy must include an understanding and appreciation of women's ways of knowing and the equalization of voice and empathy capabilities so that the power within the relationship can be shared equitably. Hare-Mustin (1998) reminded us that

> putting the needs of others first, providing understanding, and suppressing anger are not intrinsically related to gender, but to subordination. . . .What an examination of gender requirements suggests is that the therapist should hold male clients as both wounded *and* wounding. To hold men as merely wounded, as many in the men's movement have done, is to ignore hierarchies of privilege and oppression. (p. 46)

Limitations

Feminist family therapy has its limitations. The dominant discourse of feminist family therapy has been developed and practiced by White, heterosexual, middle-class to upper-class women. Not all early feminists were inclusive of all women, that is, women of color, women living in poverty, or lesbian women. They originally failed to consider that they were dominant and had privileges as White people and, at the same time, were targeted as women. With few exceptions, these White feminists did not extend their power analysis to race, class, or sexual orientation and their impact on the family until the 1990s.

"Gender is raced and classed, and shifts in meaning with age, sexual orientation, and other 'selves'" (Laird, 1998, p. 27). "A theory of gender oppression alone is insufficient to explain the multiple levels of oppression that occur in family life. Gender oppression must be viewed in the context of other oppressions with which it is embedded: racism, colonization, classism, heterosexism, and homophobia" (Almeida, Woods, Messineo, & Font, 1998, pp. 416–417). And, according to Hare-Mustin (1998), "Unless we attend to such influences, our therapy will be oppressive, not only for what it includes, but also for what it excludes" (p. 54). Greene and Boyd-Franklin (1996) described the "triple jeopardy" that African American lesbian couples face (p. 49). They are objects of gender, racial, and heterosexist institutional oppression. Consequently, they experience a range of challenges to their optimal psychological development, as do their relationships. Traditional therapeutic approaches are steeped in heterocentric and ethnocentric biases, and feminist approaches traditionally addressed only one of these biases, missing the conflicting loyalties such couples encounter.

The complex interaction of racism and sexism must be recognized within the feminist perspective. Gender power imbalances still exist among people of color, but the gender power balance between men and women of color is quite different from their White counterparts (Arnold, 1997). A feminist therapist must not only challenge obvious sexist behavior in couple relationships but also consider how racism may have contributed to the experience of power imbalance in the home. If a family of color is noticed only through the lens of gender, and racism is not considered within the assessment, an inaccurate picture of the family may emerge.

At the same time, as Raja (1998) reminded us, even though feminist discoveries and demands came from a White, middle-class, heterosexual movement, they are extremely relevant to women and men in very different life and family circumstances. Because feminist family therapy emphasizes social context, encourages advocacy for families, encourages collaborative relationships, and supports open dialogue of the family's and the therapist's values, it can be helpful in understanding the distress of women of color. Feminist family therapists should not overreact to the challenge of differences among women by forgetting about their broadly defined insights about families, their gendered division of labor, and its effect on sex inequality in all realms of life.

> The challenge . . . is to recognize both the power of universalizing women as women in the name of solidarity for social change, as well as to recognize the danger of denying or suppressing acknowledgment of differences among women. It is to learn how politically to manage fragmentation in ways that do not deny either women's differences or their interdependence. (Forcey & Nash, 1998, p. 90)

Conclusion

Feminism impacts dominant cultural values. It teaches us that we are not just products of context and culture; we shape context and culture. Feminist family therapists believe that

> a therapist [who] is not aware of gender inequities embedded in our culture and conscious of the need to change this imbalance is contributing to the problems of families and couples attempting to survive in a new and complicated world. A therapist who fails to respond to a family's presentation of their problems within a framework that takes into account the inequities of the culture, and who attempts to maintain a so-called "neutrality" vis-à-vis the family is necessarily doing sexist family therapy. (McGoldrick, Anderson, & Walsh, 1989, p. 12)

Feminist family therapists help couples and families to examine power and gender stereotyping and to move beyond the previously stigmatized meanings that the dominant culture assigns to men and women. They enable couples and families to recognize the social component of their problems and see deficiencies as a result of socialization and restricted opportunities rather than as strictly individual faults. Feminist family therapists articulate perspectives that reframe power struggles and the personalizing of differences and disclose other meanings. Although feminist family therapy focuses on many aspects of relationships within the family, it is the exploration and recognition of the gendered meanings of their behaviors, values, and patterns that produce new possibilities and options. Therapists assist families in creating a new structuring of gender relationships based on equality and partnerships.

What feminist theory offers those who are trying to develop family therapy theory is an alternative construction of reality provided by a different lens. Feminism is futurist in calling for social change and changes in both men and women. Feminist family therapy is based on a vision of equality that empowers all members of the family: men, women, and children.

References

Almeida, R., Woods, R., Messineo, T., & Font, R. (1998). The cultural context model: An overview. In M. McGoldrick (Ed.), *Re-visioning family therapy: Race, culture, and gender in clinical practice* (pp. 414–431). New York: Guilford Press.

Arnold, M. S. (1997). The connection between multiculturalism and oppression. *Counseling Today, 39*, 42.

Feldman, L. B. (1982). Sex roles and family dynamics. In F. Walsh (Ed.), *Normal family processes* (pp. 354–379). New York: Guilford Press.

Forcey, L. R., & Nash, M. (1998). Rethinking feminist theory and social work therapy. *Women and Therapy, 21*(4), 85–99.

Gilligan, C. (1982). *In a different voice.* Cambridge, MA: Harvard University Press.

Goldner, V. (1985). Feminism and family therapy. *Family Process, 24*, 31–47.

Goldner, V. (1989). Generation and gender: Normative and covert hierarchies. In M. McGoldrick, C. M. Anderson, & F. Walsh (Eds.), *Women in families: A framework for family therapy* (pp. 42–60). New York: Norton.

Goodrich, T. J., Rampage, C., Ellman, B., & Halstead, K. (1988). *Feminist family therapy: A casebook.* New York: Norton.

Greene, B., & Boyd-Franklin, N. (1996). African-American lesbian couples: Ethnocultural considerations in psychotherapy. In M. Hill & E. D. Rothblum (Eds.), *Couples therapy: Feminist perspectives* (pp. 49–60). New York: Harrington Park Press.

Hare-Mustin, R. T. (1978). A feminist approach to family therapy. *Family Process, 17*, 181–193.

Hare-Mustin, R. T. (1989). The problem of gender in family therapy theory. In M. McGoldrick, C. M. Anderson, & F. Walsh (Eds.), *Women in families: A framework for family therapy* (pp. 61–77). New York: Norton.

Hare-Mustin, R. T. (1998). Challenging traditional discourses in psychotherapy: Creating space for alternatives. *Journal of Feminist Family Therapy, 10*(3), 39–56.

Hare-Mustin, R. T., & Hines, P. M. (1978). Ethical concerns in family therapy. *Professional Psychology, 9*, 165–171.

Laidlaw, T. A., & Malmo, C. (1990). Introduction: Feminist therapy and psychological healing. In T. A Laidlaw, C. Malmo, & Associates (Eds.), *Healing voices: Feminist approaches to therapy with women* (pp. 1–11). San Francisco: Jossey-Bass.

Laird, J. (1998). Theorizing culture: Narrative ideas and practice principles. In M. McGoldrick (Ed.), *Re-visioning family therapy: Race, culture, and gender in clinical practice* (pp. 20–30). New York: Guilford Press.

McGoldrick, M., Anderson, C. M., & Walsh, F. (Eds.). (1989). *Women in families: A framework for family therapy.* New York: Norton.

Miller, J. B. (1986). *Toward a new psychology of women* (2nd ed.). Boston: Beacon Press.

Nicholson, L. (1997). The myth of the traditional family. In H. L. Nelson (Ed.), *Feminism and families* (pp. 26–42). New York: Routledge.

Parker, L. (1998). The unequal bargain: Power issues in couples therapy. *Journal of Feminist Family Therapy, 10*(3), 17–37.

Raja, S. (1998). Culturally sensitive therapy for women of color. *Women and Therapy, 21*(4), 67–84.

Rampage, C. (1998). Feminist couple therapy. In F. M. Dattilio (Ed.), *Case studies in couple and family therapy: Systemic and cognitive perspectives* (pp. 353–370). New York: Guilford Press.

Russell, M. N. (1984). *Skills in counseling women: The feminist approach.* Springfield, IL: Charles C Thomas.

Sims, J. M. (1996). The use of *voice* for assessment and intervention in couples therapy. In M. Hill & E. D. Rothblum (Eds.), *Couples therapy: Feminist perspectives* (pp. 61–77). New York: Harrington Park Press.

Skerrett, K. (1996). From isolation to mutuality: A feminist collaborative model of couples therapy. In M. Hill & E. D. Rothblum (Eds.), *Couples therapy: Feminist perspectives* (pp. 93–106). New York: Harrington Park Press.

Tong, R. (1989). Introduction: The varieties of feminist thinking. In R. Tong (Ed.), *Feminist thought: A comprehensive introduction* (pp. 1–9). San Francisco: Westview Press.

Walters, M., Carter, B., Papp, P., & Silverstein, O. (1988). *The invisible web: Gender patterns in family relationships.* New York: Guilford Press.

■ ■ ■

Women of Color and Feminist Family Counseling: Caveats

Mary Smith Arnold, PhD

The family has been contested ground for people of color in the United States since their initial contact with the West through conquest, enslavement, forced labor, colonization, and second-class citizenship. Societal protection and the idea of family as sacrosanct were benefits that were never afforded families of color. In fact, just the opposite is true. Families of color, historically, have been victims of legal and social measures that undermined their ability to nurture and provide economically for their members. Against the forces of institutionalized racism, sexism, and classism, people of color have had to fashion families that supported their physical as well as spiritual survival in a social context that ranged from benign neglect to open hostility.

Women have played distinct and crucial roles in the sustenance and maintenance of families of color (Dill, 1994). Their labor outside (productive) and inside (reproductive) the home, child-rearing practices, and the reenactment and transmission of rituals have saved whole peoples. Despite the fact that patriarchy was evident in their most personal space—their homes—women of color were and are ever conscious of the effects of racism as an all-encompassing force threatening the total life of the family.

In our work with all clients, it is essential that we as counselors consider the larger context of historical oppression (Arnold, 1997); with women of color this becomes an even greater imperative. They have been victims of and active agents against oppression since their earliest contact with European Americans. Although American Indian women, African American women, Asian American women, and Latinas share common themes resulting from multiple forms of oppression, they have unique cultural and historical experiences that make it impossible to delineate the permutations of each group's experience. Therefore, this chapter focuses on the broadest themes related to the lives of women of color and how feminist family counselors may better serve them.

Commonalities

All women in the United States suffer from the constraints imposed by a society that is constructed on the principles of valuing men over women. However, not all women suffer in the same way, at the same level, to the same degree, or even around the same aspects of inequality. The individual woman is shaped by an interplay of her own unique set of familial and personal characteristics as well as larger social forces (McGoldrick, 1998). There is no universal model in which all women should or can be patterned, that is, "one-size-fits-all." Yet all women endure the inequities of a lack of access to political, economic, and social power regardless of their awareness of these inequalities (Cook, 1993). It is clear that women of color and White women share the common ground of sexist oppression.

Typically, assumptions about all women are rooted in narrow views of patriarchy based on the lives of middle-class White women and men (Collins, 1990). Although White women and women of color are victims of sexism, the additional burdens of racism, and often class oppression, result in an elaborate layering of experiences. The result is an intricate multilayered context that requires counselors to assume a learner's posture toward individual families as well as the cultural group to which the family belongs. Counselors skilled in multiculturalism are aware that every client is unique and yet is affected by his or her cultural and sociopolitical experiences. It is like driving a car; one has to pay attention to what is immediately in front while maintaining an acute awareness of the road ahead and the lanes on either side.

Differences

Feminists have learned that honoring difference promotes a richer appreciation for one's connections and a fuller understanding of the multiple realities of women's experiences (Jordan, 1997). There are several aspects of the experiences of women of color that counselors need to be aware of when working from a feminist perspective with women and families of color. They are (a) the impact of racial stereotypes on women, (b) the saliency of racial identity, (c) the survival function of the family in the face of racism, (d) male–female relationships, and (e) the significance of community.

Racial Stereotypes

Women of color have an additional burden of negotiating racist stereotypes that further distort their own and society's image of them as women. All women are targeted by sexist stereotypes, but the intermingling of pejorative racial images intensifies and complicates identity formation for women of color (Lu, 1997; Sanders, 1996). Racist stereotypes of women of color such as "China doll," "hot tamale," "geisha girl," "Indian princess," and "hot mama" oversexualize them and further demean their worth as women. The images of women of color in society are often extreme polar opposites and one-dimensional. They are represented as silent and self-sacrificing women or as loud, immoral, streetwise whores.

What is most insidious about stereotypes is that they have the power to influence self-perceptions and behaviors (Sue & Sue, 1999). Women of color are often sensitive to these and other stereotypes and avoid behaviors and social contacts that might confirm racist and sexist stereotypes of them in the minds of others. Still some women may act out stereotypes, having internalized society's view of them. One simple example of this is associated with wearing the color red for African American women. Very dark-skinned women may avoid the color red, thinking it is unattractive against dark skin and makes them appear to be "loose women." Yet other women may wear red to highlight their sensuality and to act out society's image of them as sexually promiscuous and immoral. Clients may be hypersensitive to these stereotypes. In an effort to contradict society's view of them as "loose women," clients may adopt a reserve or pious posture that counselors might misinterpret as rigidity, aloofness, or even resistance to counseling.

Another effect of stereotypes is the blotting out of all individual uniqueness. Many times women of color express anger at how members of the majority culture in their jobs or other points of contact "don't really see them" for whom they are. They often state that Whites, and some people of color, do not look past the racial stereotypes to get to know them as human beings. Asians must be quiet and subservient; many White people, and some people of color, respond to and label assertive Asian women as atypical. They do not accept that Asian women can exhibit the full range of human expression. This same dynamic is in play with other women of color: Latinas must be emotional and sensuous; American Indians must be silent and spiritual; African Americans must be vocal and strong. Women who do not fit the mold cast for them are often viewed as lacking cultural authenticity. The dominant culture limits and defines behavior for women of color. This often results in conflictual and self-repudiating behaviors by women of color.

How can counselors help?
Clients may be extra cautious to screen for counselors who may believe or act out the dominant society's stereotypes (Sue & Sue, 1999). Counselors should be aware that women of color come into counseling with a history of being misrepresented in the popular culture. They are affected deeply by these distortions. How can counselors support women of color in erasing negative assaults to their self-image? Counselors can help by

1. Recognizing that stereotypes have grown out of the historical oppression of people of color and that they were used as a means of social control by the dominant society. Counselors should seek more accurate information about the histories of women of color.
2. Acknowledging to clients that they are aware that stereotypes are sneaky and that they may affect the counselors' thinking, but that they are consciously working to rid themselves of negative, harmful information that might get in the way of being effective helpers and just human beings.
3. Stating clearly that they are learning more about how stereotypes might affect the counseling process and indicating that they need the client's help to unravel the personal impact of stereotypes on the client's perspective of life.
4. Acknowledging that it must be hard to be a woman living in a society that does not affirm one's identity as a woman.

The Saliency of Racial Identity

Feminist family counselors who are concerned about issues of diversity will have to set aside some cherished beliefs to work successfully with women of color. These counselors must challenge and unmask major tenets of feminist thought, including the notion that gender (female and male) is a separate defining category apart from race, class, and sexual orientation. In fact, gender, just like race and class, interacts with other defining social categories such as religion, sexual orientation, and national origin. Gender has no meaning apart from race, class, and sexual orientation. All women or men do not experience gender in the same way. For women of color, gender socialization messages differ from those given to White women, especially middle-class White women, around physical attractiveness (Sanders, 1996), intellectual capabilities (Collins, 1990), and workforce participation (Davis, 1981).

Goldner (1988) helped us to understand that gender is a coequal organizing principle in the construction of family life with generation or age. Race or one's ethnic/cultural context is also an equally powerful organizing principle in the construction of family life. Families bring their social and political histories with them when they come for counseling, even when they are not consciously presenting issues from that context. In counseling, women bring the issues related to their social context; for women of color, this means the counselor must notice race, class, and sexual orientation.

Race is socially constructed (Robinson, 1999). The idea that human beings are divided into separate and distinct racial groups has been proven to have no basis in the biological sciences. However, because the United States and other parts of the world have been organized around the principle of racial differences, we have come to act as if race is *real*. Race has been used to award privilege and power to some groups and to disempower and disadvantage other groups in society (Arnold, 1997). The more than 400 years of racial oppression require that counselors not dismiss or ignore race as a factor.

For many women of color, race is their most salient social identity; all other aspects of their identity are mediated by race. Women will name their racial identification first—for example, African American or Asian American—as a prefix to the word *woman*, especially when speaking to persons outside of their cultural group, to explain or make themselves known to others. American Indian women often name their tribal nation before gender. Latinas have the advantage of a language that allows them to simultaneously identify their racial/cultural group and their gender. This does not mean that these women view themselves as women secondarily but that their view of themselves as women is shaped by the social realities of their lives in the context of a race-conscious society. The point is that gender is intricately interwoven with racial identity for women of color. Feminist theorist Vicki Spelman (as cited in Tatum, 1997) pointed out that racial identity cannot be separated from one's femaleness like "pop beads."

Increasingly, women are proudly claiming their mixed racial heritage (Williams, 1999). The population of biracial and multiracial persons is growing in the United States. Chideya (1999) suggested that the coming generation of young people will force a shift in one's thinking about racial identity. It will no longer be perceived as one or the other but as both/and, incorporating several cultural traditions. This may create an additional strain in families between generations as older family members seek to socialize their offspring into the realities of race relations, a reality that will differ greatly for the generations to come. However, this potentially new reality, based on multiracial identities among a larger share of the American population, still may not be enough to change power relationships or eliminate the deep fear residing in the American psyche about race.

How can counselors attend to race in counseling?

Whether a client claims a single racial, biracial, or multiracial identity, race has significance. Many times, race plays a part in the presenting problem or the framing of potential solutions. Counselors must surmount their own fears and discomfort in talking about race. They must be willing to explore the particular dynamics of race in every client's life. Counselors can attend to race in counseling by

1. Accepting that the presenting problem as framed by the client or the larger world may have something to do with race, although it may not always be obvious to the client or the counselor.
2. Learning about the dynamics of race in the United States and accepting that these dynamics are at play, regardless of the racial identification of the family or the counselor. Race is significant whether the counselor and the family are from the same cultural context or a cross-cultural context.
3. Reviewing and interrogating their own racial experiences, attitudes, and frameworks.

4. Appropriately disclosing their own learning process regarding the dynamics of race, contrasting earlier impressions and experiences with current ones.
5. Remaining open and willing to broach the subject of race.

The Survival Function of the Family

Although feminist theorists have clearly stated that feminism is about generating more choices for women *and* men, there is a common perception among many practitioners that leaving the family is the most direct route to liberation. Sometimes this leaving is more figurative than literal, but the encouragement to put one's self first often means turning away from the needs of the family. Despite the groundbreaking feminist research on self in relation to others (Gilligan, 1982; Miller, 1976; Surrey, 1991), relationships within families of color are often devalued and characterized as exploitive. Women of color sometimes are viewed by feminist counselors as naive about gender issues or as pathological and self-sacrificing for maintaining close family ties.

Women of color have had to sustain horrendous sacrifices to save their families from the brutalities of conquest, colonization, enslavement, unjust immigration policies, and second-class citizenship (Dill, 1994). The historical struggles of women of color to combat the oppressive assaults on family life required many unconventional responses. African American women have fostered children and re-created families by embracing "fictive kin." Chinese women raised their children while enduring long separations from their husbands, for as many as 20 or 30 years, because of discriminatory U.S. immigration policies that prohibited Chinese laborers from bringing their wives into the United States. Mexican American women coped with transience and labor market abuse as they raised their children in mining and railroad camps, and later as migrant farm laborers (Dill, 1994). American Indian women passed down tribal knowledge and suffered separation from as well as the imposition of Western education on their children by U.S. government-controlled missionary boarding schools. In most other contexts, such sacrifice would be called heroism. In a society that is hostile to families of color, maintaining one's familial connections is a form of political resistance.

The family has helped many women of color resist limiting sexual prescriptions. For example, in discussing African American women, Turner (1997) stated that "Black women have been socialized to integrate traditional *male roles* of achievement, autonomy and independence with the more traditional *female roles* of caretaking and nurturing as a 'norm'"(p. 78). Therefore, Black women often see themselves as powerful and able to competently move in a "man's world." However, Turner also suggested that this comes at a high price because attachment to the family, and by extension, the community, requires fulfilling nurturing roles. This often leads to feelings of guilt, incompetence, and divided loyalties as African American women try to satisfy the mutually exclusive demands of male and female roles.

How can counselors help?

Counselors can help by understanding the loyalty and commitment women of color have to their families. At the same time, women of color may have deep conflicting feelings regarding their roles and responsibilities within their families. Counselors can help by

1. Understanding the significance of family as a paradox for women of color.
2. Acquiring historical knowledge of widely shared familial experiences of racial/ethnic groups (e.g., the internment of Japanese Americans).
3. Giving clients permission to explore their negative feelings regarding their family, while concurrently respecting the value and strength of the family.
4. Acknowledging the daily acts of heroism it takes to maintain a family in a racist and sexist society.
5. Working from a strength rather than a deficient perspective and highlighting adaptive cultural values and survival skills.
6. Examining their own view regarding the meaning of family and how it influences their work as counselors.

Male–Female Relationships

Women of color share racist oppression with the men in their lives: their fathers, brothers, male relatives, friends, lovers, and sons. Counselors need to be aware of important aspects of the dynamics that influence male–female relationships among people of color, including (a) racial barriers that hinder men of color from performing the provider role and (b) feelings of *fear for,* and *protectiveness toward,* men of color that have been inculcated in women of color.

Racial barriers to full employment and educational opportunities persist for men of color and have a damaging effect on family life. The criminalization of men of color, especially of African Americans and Latinos, also deprives women and children of the husband and father in the home, making it harder for these families to thrive. These societal inequalities create tensions within interpersonal relationships (Collins, 1990; Dill, 1994; Sue & Sue, 1999). Further compounding this problem is the interplay of sexism and racism that consigns women of color to dead-end, low-wage jobs (Dill, 1994).

Feminists, for the most part, recognize that all men are not equally powerful in this society given race and class differences. However, many feminist family counselors do not understand the concerns of women of color regarding the safety and protection of the men in their lives. They may not understand the extent to which women of color have been socialized to be sensitive to the injustices that men experience because of race oppression. The urging by counselors to seek "help" from social service systems such as child protective service agencies, the police, health care agencies, and even schools can be viewed by women of color as turning to the very systems that caused family distress in the first place. These systems are often excessively harsh and punitive when dealing with men and boys of color.

Even in extreme cases of domestic violence, women may be reluctant to call the police. They may display ambivalence after calling the police to stop acts of violence. In addition to the second-guessing and the fears associated with such circumstances, the woman of color may also feel she has betrayed her strongest ally against oppression. There may also be an overwhelming sense of powerlessness connected to surrendering to a system that excludes and demeans people of color.

Counselors also may assume that all women can turn to the system for help. This is not true for women of color. Often they are abused or simply neglected and underserved by the network of social services designed to serve women and families. This is true regardless of class status for women of color. Racism and sexism often converge to deny women of color the most basic respect and support when they seek information or support from legal, health, civic, or educational institutions. Seeking help may actually make things worse for women of color and their families.

How can counselors help?

Counselors can help by appreciating the complexity of male–female relationships for men and women of color by

1. Seeking more information about the economic disparities that people of color endure in the United States.
2. Respecting the deep cultural bond between men and women of color.

3. Noticing the inequities within social service systems that are prejudicial against men of color.
4. Assuming the best about each client and not blaming clients for the double-bind that they find themselves in with their intimate partners because of racism and sexism.
5. Expanding their own knowledge of relationships between men and women of color.

Significance of Community

The last area of concern related to the lives of women of color that demands the attention of feminist family counselors is the significance of community. Researchers have noted a "we orientation" in people of color in comparison with the individual or "me orientation" of the dominant European American culture (Gaines, 1997). Triandis (as cited in Gaines, 1997) called the "we orientation" a collectivist spirit that is representative of an entire ethnic group. These orientations are not mutually exclusive within an individual person or an ethnic group. Persons with a collectivist orientation may be found within an individualist culture and vice versa (Gaines, 1997).

Family counselors and scholars have acknowledged the importance of social context including community. Lewis, Lewis, Daniels, and D'Andrea (1998) called for the inclusion of the family's social support network in the counseling process. Others have noted the special role counselors can play in community empowerment (Lewis & Arnold, 1998). However, counselors' practices have not incorporated community as a value (May & Church, 1999). This lag in our practices may have negative consequences for serving women of color. The socialization process for women of color inculcates a collectivist spirit that extends beyond one's immediate family. Women of color are central to promoting collectivist values within their families and communities.

It is important for feminist family counselors to recognize that the community is often a source of inspiration and a catalyst for change. Common themes among people of color are the struggle against oppression and social exclusion, the struggle for cultural survival and autonomy, and the struggle for social justice to redress past injustices. Women play a critical role in advancing social justice. Whether they are active in formal organizations or involved in informal networks for mutual aid, they are contributing to their ethnic group or community. Working in tandem with others in social organizations provides opportunities for personal growth. Working in churches and temples, schools, and cultural institutions, as well as political and civic organizations, gives women a part in shaping and sustaining the community for future generations. Community work also connects women to the historical struggle of their people.

Although family counselors are beginning to understand the two-way benefits of community as a source of inspiration and a resource for helping families, it is important to note that people of color have known this and have used the community as a healing force in their lives for generations. Counselors need to understand the values associated with a "we orientation." Feminist family counselors might misinterpret behaviors associated with the collectivist spirit as pathological or self-sacrificing in the Western or dominant cultural sense. Such counselors must understand that considering the needs of the group is as personally fulfilling and morally enhancing in the collectivist orientation as considering one's individual needs in the individualist orientation.

It is equally important for counselors to recognize that balancing group demands while living in an individualist-oriented society is difficult at best. The U.S. society is structured to support and privilege the needs of the individual. Pressures can mount, and meeting expectations of one's ethnic group can become overwhelming. Counselors need to strike a delicate balance between helping clients recognize the tensions created by possessing a "we orientation" within a "me orientation" social context. Clients who express frustration and a sense of being overwhelmed by family and community may be trying to balance the competing demands of these two orientations. However, these clients may be unwilling to shed the values of their group to respond to the values of the dominant culture. Of course, clients may not clearly articulate the conflict surrounding these issues.

How can counselors help?

Counselors can help by understanding the differences between a "we" versus a "me" orientation and developing an appreciation for both. They also can help by

1. Affirming the "we orientation" in the lives of clients and not pathologizing clients who put group needs above their individual needs.
2. Recognizing that individuals are not purely collectivist or individualist in their personal lives. Counselors should respectfully assist clients in balancing these seemingly competing cultural values.

3. Exploring their own values regarding collectivist and individualist perspectives and assessing how these values influence
   their work as counselors.
4. Noticing if clients are connected to a larger support network
   and incorporating "community" as a significant part of the therapeutic process.
5. Appreciating the complexity of the "we orientation" and accepting that for individual clients and across ethnic groups
   there are differences within this phenomenon.

Conclusion

All clients are unique with their own specific concerns intercon-
nected with the social, political, and cultural context of their environment. Therefore, women of color present in counseling with all
of the issues that result from living in a sexist society: overburdened
and undersupported by their families, physical and emotional abuse,
workplace harassment issues, alcoholism, and general feelings of
powerlessness. Minimally, these issues and others must be coupled
with the counselors' understanding of the impact of racism on the
lives of women of color. Whatever issues women of color present
in counseling, the influence of oppression from the larger social,
political, and economic context must be kept in the foreground so
that the counseling process is not detoured down a dead-end road.

References

Arnold, M. S. (1997, May). The connection between multiculturalism and
    oppression. *Counseling Today, 39,* 42.
Chideya, F. (1999). *The color of our future.* New York: Morrow.
Collins, P. H. (1990). *Black feminist thought: Knowledge, consciousness,
    and the politics of empowerment.* New York: Routledge.
Cook, E. P. (1993). *Women, relationships, and power: Implications for
    counseling.* Alexandria, VA: American Counseling Association.
Davis, A. (1981). *Women, race, and class.* New York: Random House.
Dill, B. T. (1994). Fictive kin, paper sons, and compadrazgo: Women of
    color and the struggle for family survival. In M. B. Zinn & B. T. Dill
    (Eds.), *Women of color in U.S. society* (pp.149–169). Philadelphia: Temple
    University Press.
Gaines, S. O., Jr. (1997). *Culture, ethnicity, and personal relationship
    processes.* New York: Routledge.
Gilligan, C. (1982). *In a different voice.* Cambridge, MA: Harvard Univer-
    sity Press.

Goldner, V. (1988). Generation and gender: Normative and covert hierarchies. *Family Process, 27,* 17–32.

Jordan, J. V. (Ed.). (1997). *Women's growth in diversity: More writings from the Stone Center.* New York: Guilford Press.

Lewis, J. A., & Arnold, M. S. (1998). From multiculturalism to social action. In C. C. Lee & G. R. Walz (Eds.), *Social action: A mandate for counselors* (pp. 51–65). Alexandria, VA: American Counseling Association.

Lewis, J. A., Lewis, M. D., Daniels, J. A., & D'Andrea, M. J. (1998). *Community counseling: Empowerment strategies for a diverse society.* Pacific Grove, CA: Brooks/Cole.

Lu, L. (1997). Critical visions: The representation and resistance of Asian women. In S. Shah (Ed.), *Dragon ladies: Asian American feminists breathe fire* (pp. 17–28). Boston: South End Press.

May, K. M., & Church, N. L. (1999). Families and communities: Building bridges. *The Family Journal: Counseling and Therapy for Couples and Families, 7,* 51–53.

McGoldrick, M. (Ed.). (1998). *Re-visioning family therapy: Race, culture, and gender in clinical practice.* New York: Guilford Press.

Miller, J. B. (1976). *Toward a new psychology of women.* Boston: Beacon Press.

Robinson, T. L. (1999). The intersections of dominant discourses across race, gender, and other identities. *Journal of Counseling and Development, 77,* 73–79.

Sanders, J. L. (1996). *My face holds the history of my people and the feelings in my heart: Racial socialization and evaluations of facial attractiveness of preadolescent African American girls.* Unpublished doctoral dissertation.

Sue, D. W., & Sue, D. (1999). *Counseling the culturally different: Theory and practice* (3rd ed.). New York: Wiley.

Surrey, J. (1991). The "self-in-relation": A theory of women's development. In J. V. Jordan, A. G. Kaplan, J. B. Miller, I. P. Stiver, & J. L. Surrey (Eds.), *Women's growth in connection: Writings from the Stone Center* (pp. 51–66). New York: Guilford Press.

Tatum, B. D. (1997). Racial identity development and relational theory: The case of Black women in White communities. In J. V. Jordan (Ed.), *Women's growth in diversity: More writings from the Stone Center* (pp. 91–106). New York: Guilford Press.

Turner, C. W. (1997). Clinical applications of the Stone Center theoretical approach to minority women. In J. V. Jordan (Ed.), *Women's growth in diversity: More writings from the Stone Center* (pp. 4–90). New York: Guilford Press.

Williams, C. B. (1999). Claiming a biracial identity: Resisting social constructions of race and culture. *Journal of Counseling and Development, 77,* 32–35.

3

Feminist Family Therapy: For Heterosexual Couples and Families Only?

Susan R. Seem, PhD

G ay, lesbian, and bisexual couples and families face the same issues that are encountered by nongay families. However, negotiating such issues as intimacy, commitment, and decision making often is more complicated for gay, lesbian, and bisexual families because of homophobia and heterosexism in society (Cabaj & Klinger, 1996; McCandlish, 1982). Therefore, an understanding of homophobia, internalized homophobia, and heterosexism is essential for feminist family therapists working with same-sex and bisexual couples and families.

Counseling and psychotherapy in general and family therapy in particular have diminished or ignored lesbian, gay, and bisexual issues (Goodrich, Rampage, Ellman, & Halstead, 1988; Hill & Rothblum, 1996). Feminist family therapy also has privileged heterosexual couples. "The centrality of power draws feminist therapists' attention primarily to heterosexual relationships—especially marriage, as the relationship in which the culturally prescribed power inequities between men and women have their most pernicious effects" (Rampage, 1998, p. 353). Furthermore, training programs often assume dominant notions about human relationships, and they value and teach "those experiences that are White, male, heterosexual, young, middle class, able-bodied and North American" (Brown, 1989, p. 446). Consequently, therapists often lack knowledge about gay, lesbian, and bisexual issues and may hold dominant ideas about health and pathology.

In this chapter, therapists' inherent biases are explored. Then the knowledge and sensitivity necessary to work with gay, lesbian, and bisexual couples and families are discussed. Feminist family therapy's challenge to traditional conceptualization of families and therapeutic notions of health are delineated. Finally, themes in same-sex and bisexual couples' and families' treatment are explored.

Inherent Biases

Because the dominant paradigm for relationships and family is heterosexual, it is important for feminist family therapists to examine their beliefs about families, attraction, relationships, intimacy, and parenting as they have examined power and gender. Common prejudices held about gay, lesbian, and bisexual couples and families also need to be explored (Hargaden & Llewellin, 1996). The pervasiveness of the dominant culture's stereotypes and myths about homosexuality makes it imperative that feminist family therapists become aware of their own innate homophobia and heterosexism (Brown, 1986; McDonald & Steinhorn, 1994). These innate biases may result in the following: (a) a belief that homosexuality is pathological, (b) a bias toward heterosexual behavior, (c) an underestimation of daily stresses and denial of the problems and issues particular to lesbian and gay relationships, and (d) a valuing of the Western nuclear family as the norm. Another assumption that therapists may hold is that all homosexual relationships are alike. This bias results in the denial of the uniqueness of relationships and may ignore the intersection of such factors as race/ethnicity, social class, religion, and gender with homophobia and heterosexism.

Knowledge and Sensitivity

Therapists often operate from a traditional knowledge base that is heterosexist and assume heterosexuality and heterosexual norms for relationships. For example, such a knowledge base would hold a pro-sex, sexist, and heterosexual bias that focuses on initiation and genital sex (Brown, 1988; Hall, 1996). Initiating sexual intercourse is the male prerogative, and only genital sex is the "real" sex. Equal primacy of male and female desire in heterosexual relationships would not be considered, and sex between two men or two women would be "unnatural." It would view gay and lesbian couples by only their sexual orientation and would believe that gay men and lesbian couples do not have children, do not form long-term relationships, and are inevitably alienated from their families of origin (Stein, 1996). Therefore, it is imperative that feminist family therapists learn a new knowledge base about the experience of being a gay, lesbian, or bisexual couple or family in an antihomosexual world.

To work effectively with gay, lesbian, and bisexual couples and families, therapists should have a knowledge base that does not include heterosexual preference and is inclusive of all couples and families. Therapists should possess a body of knowledge about lesbian, gay male, and bisexual identity development (Cass, 1979; Falco, 1995), stages of couple relationships (Morales, 1996), and an awareness of androcentric bias in many developmental models (Fassinger, 1991). Furthermore, therapists need to view families as small social systems that are working to meet the needs of their members while also living in an essentially hostile environment (Harry, 1988). In fact, it is important for therapists not to impose their ideas of what constitutes a relationship on their clients (Cabaj & Klinger, 1996). Additionally, therapists must have knowledge of local and national resources (Seem, 1997), understand the place of civil rights in the lives of their clients (Butler & Clarke, 1991), and be aware of the regional and sociopolitical climate effect on gay and lesbian experience (Hall, 1978). Issues of how race, culture, class, and other group memberships interact with homophobia and heterosexism are important considerations in the treatment of sexual minority couples (Brown, 1988; Pearlman, 1996). Safe-sex practices and knowledge of HIV and AIDS issues are prerequisites for therapists (Butler & Clarke, 1991).

Brown (1989) proposed three elements common to lesbian and gay reality: biculturalism, marginality, and normative creativity. These elements are important aspects of the therapist's knowledge base. Gay men and lesbians are bicultural; that is, they live simultaneously in both the nongay and the gay/lesbian cultures. This experience may create different ways of knowing and understanding oneself and one's reality that can help both therapists and lesbian, gay, and bisexual couples and families create effective and new ways of being. Marginality, or a sense of otherness, also informs gay and lesbian experience. Sense of otherness is gay men's and lesbian women's first awareness of who they are; it is experienced as "simply the vague sense of difference and distance from the rituals of the heterosexual world" (Brown, 1989, p. 450). The experience of marginality also creates new lenses from which to examine families and couples. For example, lesbians and gay men have created families that are not patriarchal (Firestone, 1970, as cited in Brown, 1989), and lesbian couples have created distinctly lesbian ways to raise children (Cooper, 1987, as cited in Brown, 1989). By the absence of clear norms about how to be gay and lesbian, gay men and lesbians have created their own norms; in fact, they have had to learn how to be gay and lesbian in a heterosexual world. Thus, normative creativity is another theme of gay and lesbian experience.

Sensitivity to and appreciation of sexual minority experience are crucial to working with same-sex and bisexual couples and families. Whether gay or lesbian or nongay, therapists must be willing to take a stand and affirm gay and lesbian couples and families. Given heterosexism and homophobia, lesbian and gay couples and families experience a lack of recognition, a lack of social acceptance, and often condemnation in the cultural mainstream (Johnson & Keren, 1995). Furthermore, they usually lack legal, religious, and familial support for their relationships; in some instances, gay couples' very existence is under attack (Cabaj & Klinger, 1996; Johnson & Keren, 1995). "Thus gay and lesbian families must constantly interact with a larger society that either ignores or devalues them and frequently tries to destroy their connections by removing their children and controlling adult relationships" (Stein, 1996, p. 505).

It is essential for therapists to appreciate the impact of both internal and external homophobia on sexual functioning (Brown, 1988). Homophobia is an irrational fear, intolerance, and hatred of gay, lesbian, and bisexual people (Pharr, 1988). It is a cultural phenomenon that manifests itself in negative stereotypes about and discrimination against gay men, lesbians, and bisexuals and their lives and relationships. Because gay, lesbian, and bisexual people are socialized in a homophobic culture, they are likely to internalize these negative stereotypes and beliefs. This introjection of negative cultural beliefs and fears about homosexuality into one's perception of self results in varying degrees of self-hatred and low self-esteem and is labeled *internalized homophobia* (Weinberg, 1972). Thus, a couple may not be sexually active because they have internalized the homophobic message that gay and lesbian sex is disgusting. Additionally, a couple might not protect the relationship from boundary violations by others because they themselves believe the homophobic stereotype that gay and lesbian relationships are sick and thus will not last. Furthermore, therapists need to monitor their awareness of their own racism, attitudes toward social class, and feelings and assumptions about interracial unions (Pearlman, 1996).

Thus, working with same-sex and bisexual couples and families calls on therapists to be aware of their own biases and prejudices and to develop a base of knowledge that accurately reflects sexual minority experience in a heterosexist and homophobic society. Most important, therapists must rearrange their norms and assumptions; in essence, they need to set aside the lens through which they have learned to view the world. Therapists' sensitivity includes the ability to be curious about dominant notions and generalizations about gay male and lesbian couples. Therapists should be flexible and possess a degree of uncertainty, curiosity, and openness to ambiguity and creativity in terms of how they and their clients view health, family, and relationships.

Feminist Family Therapy

A feminist perspective changes the lens through which family therapists traditionally view their work. This perspective "is committed to exploring and elaborating the *context* and the *process* in the formation and transformation of any human experience" (Walters, 1990, p. 51). A feminist perspective departs radically from the traditional androcentric notions about the functioning of families. It acknowledges that the "personal is political" in families and, thus, is about understanding human experience within the context of a dominant cultural climate that is White, heterosexual, male, Christian, able-bodied, and middle class. Feminist family therapists have expanded family therapy to include gender, the culture, and the sociopolitical context as crucial components in the construction and interactions of families. This viewpoint, therefore, challenges a core belief of family therapy—that the family is a system "governed by its own internal regulatory mechanism within which all interpersonal transactions can be understood" (Walters, 1990, p. 55).

Theory determines what therapists see and how they think about their clients' difficulties. Theory and its underlying assumptions can be unconscious or made conscious. For example, "if you call it a skunk, you will assume it smells" (Brown, 1994, p. 131). Or is theory fusion or cohesion? Feminist analyses of family theory lay bare its implicit heterosexist and sexist biases. Concepts such as fusion, triangulation, and boundaries, when applied without question, distort and pathologize sexual minority couples and families. Using a feminist analysis regarding the concepts of fusion, boundaries, and triangulation leads to a different set of assumptions about relationships.

Fusion

Fusion is an inherently gendered concept (Goodrich et al., 1988). Traditional gender-biased conceptualizations of mental health focus on independence, autonomy, and separation as hallmarks of a healthy personality or relationship. Thus, fusion is viewed as pathological. However, the risk in applying this concept to women, especially to lesbian women, is that women's gender role socialization trains them to be relational, to value focusing more on the other than on the self, and to ignore the self–relationship differentiation. The ability to relate in such a way is intensified with lesbian women in a relationship (Gray & Isenee, 1996; Roth, 1985). A gender analysis may result in viewing fusion as functional rather than pathological. Thus, two women who are able to engage in intense, protracted periods of relating may look fused when, in fact, they may be cohesive. Furthermore, fusion may create a relationship of trust and safety, resulting in growth or healing of one or both individuals (Anderson, 1996). Centralizing the experiences of oppressed groups in psychological theory, Brown (1989) suggested that what is normative in terms of emotional intimacy for lesbian couples may be, in fact, a healthy norm for all couples.

Boundaries and Triangles

The concepts of boundaries and triangulation are interrelated. Goodrich et al. (1988) criticized family therapy for using the concept of boundary as a prescription rather than a description. They argued that other than the incest taboo, the only reason for prescribing boundaries is to protect hierarchies in families, which is prescriptive. Thus, the concept of boundary is defined in a sociopolitical and cultural context that privileges heterosexual, White, middle-class, male viewpoints (Johnson & Keren, 1995). In fact, Goodrich et al. pointed out that traditional family therapy focuses on the strengthening of boundaries and rarely discusses times when a loosening of boundaries would be beneficial (e.g., in play, crisis, transitions, and certain groupings). Similarly, family therapy also believes that couples triangulate, that is, bring in a third person to avoid direct conflict or intimacy; consequently, triangles or threesomes are viewed as pathological.

An analysis of power allows therapists to value alternative ways of relating in families and couples. Same-sex and bisexual couples challenge traditional family therapy notions of boundaries and triangles. Because homophobia and heterosexism are inherent aspects in the context of the lives of sexual minority clients, their relationships often lack any kind of social, legal, or institutional recognition. Consequently, the boundaries of the relationship are often ignored by the cultural mainstream, and, therefore, a primary difficulty that a committed same-sex couple faces is that creation of rules regarding the relationship (Johnson & Keren, 1995). Because of the hostile and sometimes dangerous world, gay and lesbian couples often seek support in the gay and lesbian community. Depending on the location (e.g., urban vs. rural), size, and norms of the community and beliefs of the individual couple, gay and lesbian couples may appear to have loose boundaries or be involved in triangles.

Gender and power analyses reveal the role that female gender role socialization and women's lack of real power in the world may play in lesbian couples' difficulty with conflict. Thus, the existence of triangulation in a lesbian couple should not automatically be attributed to difficulty in resolving conflict (Goodrich et al., 1988). In fact, Goodrich et al. suggested that bringing one or more people into a conflict does not make it less direct and may in fact allow for resolution of the conflict. Involving other related parties in the conflict may be a way to diffuse the intensity of anger. Thus, anger is managed in such a way as to not destroy the relationships among the people involved in the conflict. Furthermore, just because male couples may engage in sex outside the relationship does not mean that they suffer from loose boundaries, are disengaged emotionally, or are triangulated (Johnson & Keren, 1995). The issue of sexual exclusivity exists on a continuum for male couples and depends on the norms of the gay community and the couple's desires. Analyses of gender and power also identify the heterosexist assumptions about sexual monogamy (e.g., that nonmonogamy is an indication of poor couple functioning) and emotional disengagement (e.g., that gay men triangulate a third party or parties into relationships to avoid intimacy). These assumptions are based on the belief that heterosexuality is the only legitimate form of sexual identification in which monogamy is the norm and any other type of relating is seen as deviant.

Therapist Use of Self

A feminist analysis requires that family therapists be aware of how their gender and their use of power affect the therapy process

(Anderson, 1996; Goodrich et al., 1988). The concept of the use of the self entails the use of the therapist's gendered self (Brown, 1994; Goodrich et al., 1988). Feminist family therapists are aware that their behaviors will either support or challenge the couple's or family's beliefs about gender and gender role. Goodrich et al. argued that an important goal of the use of a gendered self is to model alternatives to constricted definitions of femininity and masculinity that clients may bring to therapy.

A feminist viewpoint recognizes the power that is inherent in the role of therapist. Feminist family therapists do not want to replicate hierarchical or oppressive relationships in therapy (Hill & Rothblum, 1996). Consequently, they mutually negotiate treatment goals with their clients. In addition, feminist family therapists remain vigilant to the potential to abuse their power through the application to their clients of dominant notions of health and psychopathology. Finally, therapeutic relationships developed by feminist family therapists are those in which clients experience therapists as honest, unprejudiced, understanding, tolerant, cooperative, safe, unshockable, and democratic (Anderson, 1996; Goodrich et al., 1988).

Feminist therapists use self-disclosure as a way to reduce the artificial hierarchical boundaries that exist between therapists and clients. What therapists communicate about their sexual orientation is more important than their actual sexual orientation (Anderson, 1996). The use of self-disclosure of sexual orientation can provide an opportunity for therapists and couples or families to discuss the meaning of such information and assumptions that may result.

The notion of political action on the part of therapists is unique to feminist therapy. Brown (1988) argued that social activism is particularly important in feminist therapy with gay and lesbian clients. This stance can be extrapolated to feminist family therapists working for legal rights for gay men and lesbians. Political action by feminist family therapists connects the personal (e.g., presenting problems of sexual minority couples and families) with the political (e.g., homophobic and heterosexist society) and addresses the need to transform the hostile and oppressive environment.

Joining and Developing Rapport

Given the social and political context, same-sex couples and families are likely to expect their therapist to hold homophobic and heterosexist bias or have internalized those biases. Thus, creating a therapeutic alliance is especially crucial with gay, lesbian, and bisexual couples and families. There are a number of ways therapists can join and develop rapport with their clients. First, therapists must be a voice and a witness for lesbian and gay couples and families in a culture that at best ignores and at worst denies and condemns their existence (Johnson & Keren, 1995). Therapists can be a powerful presence that sanctions the relationship; in fact, therapists are often the only ones who validate the relationship (Krestan & Bepko, 1980). Furthermore, therapists need to normalize the experiences of same-sex and bisexual couples and families. A respectful and nonjudgmental therapeutic stance also allows for joining and the building of rapport. This stance may be conveyed in a variety of ways. Communication of gay affirmative services can be done by the inclusion of gay, lesbian, and bisexual material in the therapist's office. For example, having books that address gay, lesbian, and bisexual issues and pictures that acknowledge homosexuality will let clients know that the therapist is sensitive to such issues. In addition, therapists need to be aware of language use and their assumptions about psychological functioning (Seem, 1997). The inappropriate use of words such as *friend* rather than *partner* or *lover* sends a strong message to gay and lesbian clients. Because of internal homophobia, gay and lesbian clients may pathologize their relationship. If this is the case, it is up to the therapist to point out the strengths of the relationship and to confirm the legitimacy of the relationship. Finally, feminist therapists work with couples and families to develop mutually agreed-on goals. This process conveys the therapist's respect for the couple or family and his or her belief in the couple's or family's ability to know what is best for them.

In summary, it is crucial for feminist family therapists to join with gay, lesbian, and bisexual couples and families. Joining can be facilitated by the therapist's conveyance of his or her knowledge and sensitivity about homosexuality. Most important, therapists need to validate and affirm gay, lesbian, and bisexual relationships. Goodrich et al. (1988) and Pearlman (1996) provide case examples of feminist family therapy with lesbian couples.

Assessment in Feminist Family Therapy

Lesbian couples seeking therapy as a rule complain about difficulty in maintaining boundaries, expressing anger, avoiding fusion, and initiating and acting in both nonsexual and sexual arenas (Cabaj & Klinger, 1996; Gray & Isenee, 1996; Klinger, 1996). Gay male couples in therapy commonly complain about difficulty in maintaining rela-

tionships, overly tight boundaries, blocks to intimacy, and problems in expression of tender feelings (Brown, 1988; Cabaj & Klinger,
1996; Gray & Isenee, 1996). Although a couple may appear to be
struggling with typical concerns, it is essential that feminist family
therapists are open to viewing the couple or family as it presents
itself and maintain a nonjudgmental stance, free of heterosexist bias,
regarding relationships. The following are general areas of assessment pertinent for feminist family therapists working with same-
sex and bisexual couples and families.

Understand the impact of homophobia and heterosexism.
It is important that therapists understand and communicate the
impact of homophobia and heterosexism on couple and family functioning. Homophobia was defined earlier. Heterosexism is homophobic prejudices supported by institutional and cultural power; it is
the belief in the intrinsic superiority and rightful dominance of
heterosexuality (Lorde, 1983).

The effect of living in a hostile environment that denies gay, lesbian, and bisexual couples and families social and legal recognition
must be assessed (Brown, 1986; Stein, 1996). For example, how does
cultural and internal homophobia affect the couple's sexual functioning or ability to make a long-term commitment? How might these
factors be played out in a couple's behavior, for example, resulting
in what looks like fusion or boundary difficulties? In addition, what
is the quality of support that gay or lesbian couples or families feel?
Green, Bettinger, and Zacks (1996) suggested assessing for size, fre-
quency, and type of contact with support system, types of activities
engaged in with support system, the density of the support system
(e.g., the extent to which individuals in the system know and support each other), multisetting versus single-setting ties with support
system members, types of support, reciprocity of support, and families of choice. Finally, a feminist analysis of heterosexist privilege in
society would help couples and families understand that they are
not "flaunting" themselves when they speak of their relationships or
hurting their families by coming out (Brown, 1988). According to
Brown, heterosexist privilege allows nongays to flaunt their heterosexuality on a daily basis and makes coming out to one's family of
origin be viewed as hurtful rather than as a desire for more intimacy.

Attend to the ways in which context has shaped the meaning of behavior.
Diversity within sexual orientation requires that therapists recognize and consider bicultural and multicultural identities (Hays,

1996). When family members are from different cultures, value conflicts may occur within the system. Furthermore, therapists need to assess for culture-related strengths (e.g., extended family networks, including nonbiological networks, religious faith, and community). A feminist perspective requires that therapists understand that the source of difficulty may be located in the cultural milieu. However, attending to the sociopolitical and cultural environment's impact on family functioning does not negate the need to assess for individual pathology.

Assess gender role socialization.

Feminist family therapists have stressed the imperative of assessing the effects of gender role socialization and stereotypes on the presenting problems of heterosexual families. This assessment is as important for lesbian, gay, and bisexual families as well. However, this assessment cannot be based on heterosexual norms. Applying heterosexual norms to the lives of lesbians and gay men is called gender straightjacketing (Green et al., 1996). Female gender role socialization is suggested to result in the tendency for lesbian couples to fuse (Burch, 1986; Gray & Isenee, 1996). Conversely, male gender role socialization is thought to result in fear of intimacy for gay male couples, which results in disengagement (Gray & Isenee, 1996). However, Green et al. disputed this view. Their research suggests that lesbian couples are cohesive rather than fused and male couples are engaged rather than disengaged. They argued that lesbians and gay men are viewed as fused or disengaged because of the assumption of homosexual–heterosexual gender role equivalence.

Brown (1988) suggested that an analysis of gender role socialization creates an opportunity to examine and question the legitimacy of homophobic and sexist gender role stereotypes:

> Assessment of the rigidity of a lesbian or gay client's gender role socialization, and exploration of the penalties for gender role deviance contained within that socialization process is thus essential with sexual minority clients. The interaction of sexism, in the form of rigid gender roles, with homophobia becomes another important point of focus. (p. 213)

In many aspects of North American culture, as well as other cultures, a blurring of the differentiation between sexual orientation and gender role exists (Brown, 1988). Consequently, this blurring results in the erroneous assumption that masculine-appearing women and feminine-appearing men are homosexuals and also may result in discomfort for some gay men and lesbians about the degree of conformity to gender roles. Gender role assessment is important in order to tease out what relational problems are due to individual difficulties and what are due to rigid gender role socialization. In addition, it is important to assess a gay male couple's adherence to the male gender role socialization and the power and privilege afforded men in the dominant culture that may be interfering with the emotional functioning of their relationship (Johnson & Keren, 1995).

Attend to the gay and lesbian community.

The lesbian and gay community is an important contextual aspect to take into consideration in the assessment process. Connection to and size of the gay and lesbian community can have an impact on couples and families (Harry, 1988). For example, what kind of involvement, if any, does a couple or family have with the gay or lesbian community? Furthermore, size of the community may play an important role in understanding a couple's difficulty. For example, a small lesbian community in which all members know each other and spend time together may result in a couple having difficulty separating after a breakup. Finally, therapists need knowledge of the norms of the gay and lesbian community to have a contextual understanding of a couple's behavior. For example, some gay and lesbian communities have a norm of nonmonogamy rather than monogamy.

Respect the coming-out process.

Understanding where each individual is in the system and where the system itself is in regards to coming out is essential (Mattison & McWhiter, 1995). Internal and external homophobia may influence the where and the when of a couple's decision regarding coming out as a couple. If the cause is external homophobia, then the couple can negotiate the when and the where of coming out. However, if the cause is internal homophobia, the couple needs help in understanding how they were taught to participate in their own oppression (Brown, 1988). Furthermore, Green et al. (1996) challenged some family therapists' belief that there is a connection between relations in family of origin and relations in the couple, or that being closeted within family of origin is a form of cutoff that contributes to difficulty in the relationship. They stated that many gay or lesbian couples appear to conduct their lives quite well despite minimal or conflictual contact with families of origin.

Feminist Strategies

Although strategies used by feminist family therapists differ depending on their theoretical orientation, there are universal tools that are helpful when working with sexual minority couples and families. A few of these strategies are described from a feminist perspective that keeps analyses of gender and power in mind.

First and foremost, feminist family therapists must help clients understand how they have been taught to cooperate in their own oppression (Brown, 1988). This means helping clients deconstruct their thinking by challenging the learned description of their relationship as pathological (Simon, 1996). Deconstruction of thinking entails an examination of both homophobia and heterosexist privilege. Therapists can help clients learn and identify social norms that are oppressive. For example, couples with sexual difficulties can be helped to understand the effect of both internal and external homophobia on their sexual functioning (Brown, 1986, 1988). Therapists also can help couples understand how living in an antihomosexual world may result in the belief that their relationships will not work and, consequently, in their failure to protect their relationship. In addition, therapists can use a feminist analysis of gender and power to help clients examine heterosexist privilege that operates to ignore, deny, or distort the relationships of sexual minorities.

The deconstruction of oppression also entails the examination of gender role socialization. The task is to separate the concept of "normal and healthy" from sexist gender role norms and to provide education about the lack of usefulness of gender role stereotypes for sexual and relationship behaviors (Brown, 1988). Therapists can help couples search for exceptions to traditional gender role practices and validate the pioneering aspects of this type of endeavor (Johnson & Keren, 1995; Simon, 1996).

Another aspect of oppression is racism. It is helpful for therapists to take a sociocultural perspective that addresses race, gender, culture, and class. Therapists must help clients understand their history of discrimination of their racial/ethnic group (Greene & Boyd-Franklin, 1996). Each member of the couple or family needs to understand her or his own oppression. Furthermore, both partners need to understand their perceptions of the limitations they experience from the dominant culture and from within their own communities. Normalizing cultural differences is helpful because it points to the strength of the relationship that has held the couple together, despite differences, in a homophobic environment (Johnson & Keren, 1995).

Teaching about such family therapy concepts as boundaries and fusion from a feminist therapy perspective with distinctions made for gay and lesbian experience can help couples understand their relational struggles (Goodrich et al., 1988). This education involves helping couples distinguish between positive and negative aspects of interpersonal connectedness (Gray & Isenee, 1996; Green et al., 1996). Discussions about the influence of gender role socialization on boundary maintenance and fusion help couples create different ways of thinking about their relationships. Because homophobia and heterosexism deny sexual minority couples formal, and often any, recognition, couples need support in the development of rituals that could help them define and affirm the boundaries of their relationship. Therapists need to address the legal vulnerability of same-sex and bisexual couples and families for two reasons (Johnson & Keren, 1995). First, gay men and lesbian women are denied the legal and emotional recognition of marriage, thus asking about legal vulnerability supports a couple's boundaries. Second, couples also need awareness about living-together contracts, durable powers of attorney, wills, and living wills so that, in case of an emergency, the partner will have rights in situations in which there would normally be none.

Sometimes, gay male and lesbian couples identify themselves publicly through social activism and protest. Therapists need to describe such behaviors as acts of courage (Johnson & Keren, 1995). Negative reactions can come from many places, such as family of origin and workplace, and may impact the couple's relationship. Understanding this can help couples manage any upheaval in their lives that may be a result of social activism.

In summary, effective strategies entail helping same-sex and bisexual couples and families articulate their voice and gain knowledge about themselves rather than accept the beliefs and assumptions of the dominant oppressive culture. Such articulation and knowledge help sexual minorities create their own rules and norms, free of oppression and dominant notions, for healthy relating.

Themes in Treatment of Sexual Minority Couples and Families

There are several themes that commonly emerge in therapy with lesbian, gay male, and bisexual couples and families. Although discussed separately, the themes are interdependent, informing and transforming each other. One of the most critical themes in working with lesbian, gay, and bisexual families is how homophobia and heterosexism render them invisible in many ways. Because this theme has been stressed throughout this chapter, its impact is now assumed. However, the interaction and influence of cultural determinants such as race/ethnicity, social class, religion, and other demographic variables with homophobia and gender role socialization are further clarified.

Impact of Culture

For many people of color, culture is as crucial or even more central to identity than is a lesbian or gay identity (Greene & Boyd-Franklin, 1996; Johnson & Keren, 1995). Many sexual minority people of color experience the gay and lesbian community as racist and their families and communities as sanctuaries from racism in the dominant culture and in the gay and lesbian culture (Brown, 1988; Johnson & Keren, 1995). Therefore, coming out to families and communities may have different meanings to sexual minorities of color than to their White counterparts (Greene & Boyd-Franklin, 1996; Johnson & Keren, 1995; Morales, 1996). For example, a norm for the dominant gay men's culture is that one's sexual orientation should be known in most, if not all, areas of life (Johnson & Keren, 1995). However, for gay men in different racial/ethnic and class contexts, this idea makes little sense. For example, coming out in an Asian American family could bring shame on the family because it violates the cultural dictate that sexuality is not discussed (Chan, as cited in Johnson & Keren, 1995). Additionally, a gay Latino man coming out risks alienation from his ethnic group and family because the idea of a gay man is a contradiction in a culture that believes that men by definition are masculine (Morales, 1996).

African American lesbians must negotiate the triple discrimination of racism and homophobia in the dominant culture and sexism and homophobia in their families and communities (Greene & Boyd-Franklin, 1996). African American lesbians may be reluctant to reveal their sexual orientation because heterosexuality is the only privileged status they hold because of racism and sexism. Because of internalized racism, some African Americans may view noncompliance to traditional gender role behavior as a negative indictment of all African Americans. Cultures also differ in how they view homosexuality. Some cultures prohibit homosexuality, others forbid any open discussion about sexuality, whereas still others view homosexuality as a White phenomenon completely incompatible with minority culture identity (Johnson & Keren, 1995).

Interracial relationships face multiple challenges. Interracial lesbian couples experience increased visibility that may make them more identifiable as a couple than two people from the same racial group (Greene & Boyd-Franklin, 1996). Interracial gay male couples can also experience this increased visibility, which may result in homophobic reactions from the family of origin and the larger world. Not only must interracial couples address homophobia but they must also deal with racism. Greene and Boyd-Franklin addressed the awareness of racism and the coping strategies for dealing with racism that lesbians of color have learned. However, a White lesbian in an interracial couple may not be aware of the occurrence of racism, much less know how to cope with racism. Consequently, differing or ongoing experiences with racism can have an impact on a couple. Johnson and Keren (1995) delineated how race and class prejudice in the gay/lesbian community may result in interracial gay couples' isolation from such a community. This isolation, they believe, can threaten the couple's relationship because it lacks external support. Additionally, issues of power and privilege, expectations around visibility, and where and how support will be sought may need to be negotiated with male couples of differing cultures and races (Johnson & Keren, 1995).

Differences in social class may also affect a couple (Pearlman, 1996). Because class can act as a shield, upper-class White lesbians and gay men may find themselves less affected by homophobia (Brown, 1988). Thus, couples from different social classes may have differing experiences with homophobia and discordant expectations about coming out.

Gender Role Socialization

Family therapy and couples literature discusses how traditional gender role socialization affects women and men and how this effect is intensified in same-sex relationships (Burch, 1986; Cabaj & Klinger, 1996; Gray & Isenee, 1996). The effect of gender role stereotyping on same-sex pairs was discussed earlier. Therapists need to help clients move beyond gender role expectations and to see the strength in their noncompliance. Norms for gay men and lesbians must be understood in a nonheterosexual context. Involving another party in the relationship, for example, does not necessarily mean triangulation or disengagement. Furthermore, lesbian couples may demonstrate healthy emotional connection rather than fusion (Green et al., 1996), and gay male couples may possess a style of relatedness that is different from female relatedness but that is no less intimate and caring (Johnson & Keren, 1995).

Absence of Role Models and Cultural History

Because they live in a heterosexual environment, sexual minorities have almost no role models or cultural history to guide them in the development and maintenance of their relationships (Simon, 1996; Stein, 1996). Lesbians, gay men, and bisexual men and women are raised by nongays and lack marriage manuals and models in the public media (Decker, 1984). Therefore, same-sex and bisexual couples and families live in a world in which sexual minorities who do develop successful relationships are not readily known. This lack of role models results in the fact that gay men, lesbians, and bisexual couples must create their own rules and norms for healthy functioning. This can be a challenge in a hostile environment.

Coming Out

The stress that results from either one or the other partner revealing his or her sexual orientation is a factor that is unique to same-sex and bisexual couples and families. Coming out or "acknowledging oneself as a homosexual, and from there, letting various others know, is a difficult process which never ends as long as one is living in a heterosexual world where the assumption is that one is straight" (Decker, 1984, p. 45).

Coming out entails both individuals within the relationship accepting their stigmatized identity and the couple experiencing external pressure to keep their identity a secret (Decker, 1984). Thus, coming out may result in conflict and anxiety within the relationship. For those individuals who are on different timetables regarding the coming-out process, one member's slower or faster place can place a strain on the relationship or family. For example, a partner who is moving more quickly in the coming-out process may interpret the slower moving partner as not caring or lacking commitment to the relationship and vice versa (Decker, 1984; Roth, 1985). This asynchrony in coming out can have a profound impact on the functioning of the system and must be respected and negotiated by all members.

Family of Origin

Debate exists in the literature about the value of sexual minority clients coming out to their families of origin. Intergenerational family therapists believe there is a causal relationship between an individual's relationship with family of origin and the relationship in the couple; thus, not coming out to family of origin is believed to result in distance regulation problems (Green et al. 1996; Johnson & Keren, 1995). However, research indicates that distance in relationships with family of origin does not necessarily negatively affect the functioning of same-sex relationships (Green et al., 1996; Johnson & Keren, 1995). Thus, family-of-origin issues must be addressed on an individual, couple, and family basis.

As mentioned earlier, coming out to family of origin has different meanings for White and minority gay men and lesbians. Because of the centrality of families in some cultures and the haven from racism families provide, coming out to families of origin for minority gay men and lesbian couples may be accompanied by high levels of stress and anxiety. A gay Latino typically fears, for example, rejection and family ostracism because of the cultural value of *machismo* (e.g., as a male figure, he is expected to protect the family from harm, but coming out is seen as harmful to family; Morales, 1996). Because of the importance of family, an African American family of origin may be reluctant to exile their lesbian daughter from the family; however, their tolerance for her sexual orientation is often based on her silence (Greene & Boyd-Franklin, 1996).

Relationships with family of origin may result in boundary problems for sexual minority couples and families. For example, families of origin can invalidate or intrude into a couple's relationship (Johnson & Keren, 1995; Krestan & Bepko, 1980). Often the same-sex couple's relationship is accorded less status in the family, as are sibling heterosexual relationships. Differences in the coming-out process to family of origin and issues with competing loyalties between the relationship and family of origin can affect the couple's functioning.

Because of homophobia and heterosexism, gay men and lesbians define family in a number of different ways that extend beyond blood connections (Johnson & Keren, 1995). These families of creation typically involve close friends who provide the support, validation, and celebration of the couple's boundaries. Therapists should acknowledge and affirm such families.

Breaking Up

Breaking up a relationship is qualitatively different for gay men, lesbians, and bisexual couples than for their nongay counterparts. Roth (1985) outlined four reasons why lesbians sometimes stay in relationships that are no longer working. First, lesbians may remain in a relationship because of fear that the breakup supports the dominant culture's belief that sexual minority relationships do not last. Second, the invisibility of the lesbian population make it difficult to find another partner. Third, because of lack of legal protection for the parenting bond, lesbians who are parenting together may be reluctant to separate. Finally, when a relationship has been a secret, a lesbian is denied the comfort and acceptance that is afforded her nongay counterpart who loses a partner. These reasons seem applicable to gay men also. However, Roth proposed two reasons unique to the breakup of a lesbian couple. Breaking up challenges female gender role socialization with its expectation that women nurture relationships. The lesbian community can also be a complicating factor in the breakup of a lesbian couple. It is typical that former partners are part of the same lesbian community. As such, this continuing friendship can lead to difficulties in a new relationship. However, this involvement in the same network can result in a continuity of connection in which former partners become long-term family friends.

The following six questions, which address the themes discussed above, are offered as a guide for the exploration of contextual determinants that have an impact on gay male couples' boundary creation and maintenance. Although these questions were developed specifically for gay male couples, they are applicable, with a few changes in wording, to lesbian and bisexual couples and sexual minority families.

1. How does *male gender role socialization* affect the couple's boundaries?
2. How do relationships with the *family of creation* and *the gay/lesbian community* affect couple boundaries?
3. How do gay cultural *norms regarding sexuality* impact on couple boundaries?
4. How do relationships with *family of origin* influence the nature of the couple's boundaries?
5. What role do *ethnicity and culture* play in shaping the couple's boundaries?
6. What is the impact of *homophobia*—internal and external—on male couple boundaries? (Johnson & Keren, 1995, p. 68)

In summary, there are common themes in the treatment of sexual minority couples and families. These themes indicate the qualitatively different experience of being gay, lesbian, or bisexual in a dominantly hostile environment. Awareness of the interaction of these themes is vital to the work of feminist family therapists.

There are many other issues that are qualitatively different for gay, lesbian, and bisexual families than for heterosexual families. Among these issues are parenting, religion, HIV/AIDS, and violence. A discussion of these issues is beyond the scope of this chapter; however, their potential importance in the lives of sexual minority clients cannot be overestimated. Feminist family therapists who work with gay, lesbian, and bisexual couples and families have an ethical obligation to educate themselves about these and other issues to ensure their counseling is void of heterosexual bias.

Conclusion

In conclusion, the literature on feminist family therapy with gay men, lesbians, and bisexual couples and families is sparse. Feminist family therapists, however, can be effective in their work if they develop sensitivity for and gain knowledge about sexual minorities. Furthermore, it is imperative that feminist family therapists educate themselves about the heterosexist bias inherent in family therapy theory and practice as they have educated themselves about sexist bias. Analysis of gender and power along with an understanding of the common themes in the lives of lesbian, gay, and bisexual couples and families will help feminist family therapists practice in a way that validates and affirms sexual minorities. Perhaps, feminist family therapists can have the most impact if they are socially and politically active in order to transform the heterosexist and sexist society to one that values and celebrates the relationships and families of all people.

References

Anderson, S. C. (1996). Addressing heterosexist bias in the treatment of lesbian couples with chemical dependency. In J. Laird & R.-J. Green (Eds.), *Lesbians and gays in couples and families* (pp. 316–340). San Francisco: Jossey-Bass.

Brown, L. S. (1986). Confronting internalized oppression in sex therapy with lesbians. *Journal of Homosexuality, 12*, 99–107.

Brown, L. S. (1988). Feminist therapy with lesbians and gay men. In M. A. Dutton-Douglas & L. E. A. Walker (Eds.), *Feminist psychotherapies: Integration of therapeutic and feminist systems* (pp. 206–227). Norwood, NJ: Ablex.

Brown, L. S. (1989). New voices, new visions. *Psychology of Women Quarterly, 13*, 445–458.

Brown, L. S. (1994). *Subversive dialogues: Theory in feminist therapy.* New York: Basic Books.

Burch, B. (1986). Psychotherapy and the dynamics of merger in lesbian couples. In T. S. Stein & C. J. Cohen (Eds.), *Contemporary perspectives on psychotherapy with lesbians and gay men* (pp. 57–71). New York: Plenum.

Butler, M., & Clarke, J. (1991). Couple therapy with homosexual men. In D. Hooper & W. Dryden (Eds.), *Couple therapy: A handbook* (pp. 196–296). Philadelphia: Open University Press.

Cabaj, R. P., & Klinger, R. L. (1996). Psychotherapeutic interventions with lesbian and gay couples. In R. P. Cabaj & T. S. Stein (Eds.), *Textbook of homosexuality and mental health* (pp. 495–501). Washington, DC: American Psychiatric Press.

Cass, V. C. (1979). Homosexual identity formation: A theoretical model. *Journal of Homosexuality, 4*, 219–235.

Decker, B. (1984). Counseling gay and lesbian couples. *Journal of Social Work and Human Sexuality, 2*(3), 39–52.

Falco, K. L. (1995). Therapy with lesbians: The essentials. *Psychotherapy in Private Practice, 13*(4), 69–83.

Fassinger, R. (1991). The hidden minority: Issues and challenges working with lesbian women and gay men. *The Counseling Psychologist, 19*, 157–176.

Goodrich, T. J., Rampage, C., Ellman, B., & Halstead, K. (1988). *Feminist family therapy: A casebook.* New York: Norton.

Gray, D., & Isenee, R. (1996). Balancing autonomy and intimacy in lesbian and gay relationships. In C. J. Alexander (Ed.), *Gay and lesbian mental health: A sourcebook for practitioners* (pp. 95–114). New York: Harrington Park Press.

Green, R.-J., Bettinger, M., & Zacks, E. (1996). Are lesbian couples fused and gay male couples disengaged? In J. Laird & R.-J. Green (Eds.), *Lesbians and gays in couples and families* (pp. 185–230). San Francisco: Jossey-Bass.

Greene, B., & Boyd-Franklin, N. (1996). African-American lesbian couples: Ethnocultural considerations in psychotherapy. In M. Hill & E. D. Rothblum (Eds.), *Couples therapy: Feminist perspectives* (pp. 49–60). New York: Haworth Press.

Hall, M. (1978). Lesbian families: Cultural and clinical issues. *Social Work, 23*, 380–385.

Hall, M. (1996). Unsexing the couple. In M. Hill & E. D. Rothblum (Eds.), *Couples therapy: Feminist perspectives* (pp. 1–11). New York: Haworth Press.

Hargaden, H., & Llewellin, S. (1996). Lesbian and gay parenting issues. In D. Davies & C. Neal (Eds.), *Pink therapy: A guide for counselors and therapists working with lesbian, gay and bisexual clients* (pp. 116–130). Philadelphia: Open University Press.

Harry, J. (1988). Some problems of gay/lesbian families. In C. S. Chilman, E. W. Nunally, & F. M. Fox (Eds.), *Variant family forms* (pp. 96–113). Newbury Park, CA: Sage.

Hays, R. D. (1996). Cultural considerations in couples therapy. In M. Hill & E. D. Rothblum (Eds.), *Couples therapy: Feminist perspectives* (pp. 13–23). New York: Haworth Press.

Hill, M., & Rothblum, E. D. (Eds.). (1996). *Couples therapy: Feminist perspectives.* New York: Haworth Press.

Johnson, T. W., & Keren, M. S. (1995). Boundary creation and maintenance in male couples. *Journal of Feminist Family Therapy, 7*(3–4), 65–86.

Klinger, R. L. (1996). Lesbian couples. In R. P. Cabaj & T. S. Stein (Eds.), *Textbook of homosexuality and mental health* (pp. 339–352). Washington, DC: American Psychiatric Press.

Krestan, J., & Bepko, C. S. (1980). The problem of fusion in lesbian relationships. *Family Process, 19,* 227–289.

Lorde, A. (1983). There is no hierarchy of oppressions. *Interracial Books for Children, 14*(3–4), 9.

Mattison, A. M., & McWhiter, D. P. (1995). Lesbians, gay men, and their families. *Psychiatric Clinic of North American, 18,* 123–137.

McCandlish, B. M. (1982). Therapeutic issues with lesbian couples. In J. C. Gonsiorek (Ed.), *A guide to psychotherapy with lesbian and gay clients* (pp. 71–78). New York: Harrington Park Press.

McDonald, H. B., & Steinhorn, A. I. (1994). Counseling gay men and lesbians and their families. In J. L. Ronch, W. Van Oraum, & N. C. Stilwell (Eds.), *The counseling sourcebook: A practical reference on contemporary issues* (pp. 146–156). New York: Crossroads.

Morales, E. (1996). Gender roles among Latino gay and bisexual men. In J. Laird & R.-J. Green (Eds.), *Lesbians and gays in couples and families* (pp. 272–297). San Francisco: Jossey-Bass.

Pearlman, S. F. (1996). Loving across race and class divides: Relational challenges and the interracial lesbian couple. In. M. Hill & E. D. Rothblum (Eds.), *Couples therapy: Feminist perspectives* (pp. 25–35). New York: Haworth Press.

Pharr, S. (1988). *Homophobia: A weapon of sexism.* Little Rock, AR: Chardon.

Rampage, C. (1998). Feminist couple therapy. In F. M. Dattilio (Ed.), *Case studies in couple and family therapy: Systemic and cognitive perspectives* (pp. 353–370). New York: Guilford Press.

Roth, S. (1985). Psychotherapy with lesbian couples: Individual issues, female socialization, and the social context. *Journal of Marital and Family Therapy, 11,* 273–286.

Seem, S. R. (1997). Invisible youth: Counseling gay and lesbian adolescents. *Journal for the Professional Counselor, 12*(2), 45–53.

Simon, G. (1996). Working with people in relationships. In D. Davies & C. Neal (Eds.), *Pink therapy: A guide for counselors and therapists working with lesbian, gay and bisexual clients* (pp. 101–115). Philadelphia: Open University Press.

Stein, T. (1996). Lesbian, gay, and bisexual families. In R. P. Cabaj & T. S. Stein (Eds.), *Textbook of homosexuality and mental health* (pp. 503–511). Washington, DC: American Psychiatric Press.

Walters, M. (1990). A feminist perspective in family therapy. In M. P. Mirkin (Ed.), *The social and the political contexts of family therapy* (pp. 51–67). Boston: Allyn & Bacon.

Weinberg, G. (1972). *Society and the healthy homosexual.* New York: St. Martin's Press.

4

Feminist Family Therapy and the Male Perspective

A. Zaidy MohdZain, PhD

A common erroneous assumption regarding a feminist family therapy approach is that it is profemale and, by default, anti-male (Elliot, 1999). A feminist family therapy approach does not seek to replace male domination over women with female domination over men, nor does it seek to exclude men or isolate women from men (Elliot, 1999). The approach, however, seeks to remedy the prevailing inequality in people's daily lives, which contributes to a variety of life and adjustment stresses and issues. Instead of making choices based on stereotypical gender roles promoted by society, the approach empowers clients, male and female, to make choices consistent with their personal skills and interests and liberates them from confining cultural norms. With emphases placed on gender and power issues, the goal of feminist family therapy is the realization of fairness and equality for all, the inclusion of which benefits all—men and women (Costa & Sorenson, 1993; Elliot, 1999).

It is difficult, if not impossible, to describe what it is to be a man or a woman. Gender, being the most basic issue of diversity (Worden & Worden, 1998), is one of the powerful elements responsible for how people shape or define their self-concept and worldview (Stevens-Smith, 1995; Worden & Worden, 1998). Its pervasiveness provides us all with a lens that dictates how we view ourselves, how others view us, and how we interact with our surroundings. The gender issue is more than simply a women's issue and should not be seen as "for women only," any more than multicultural issues should be seen as "for minorities only" (Dupuy, Ritchie, & Cook, 1994; Hoffman, 1996). Gender roles are constructed socially through a complex interplay of an individual's biological, physical, psychological, and emotional development interacting with surrounding social and cultural norms (Meth, 1990). Once constructed, these gender roles are held and reinforced to the degree that they become a form of belief system or reality. The differing gender roles for men and women require strict conformance with their own rules and limits (Myers, 1999). Myers stated that the stereotypical polarized socialization process dictates that adherence to one specific gender role means avoidance of the other gender role. Adherence to and avoidance of these strict norms both restrain and control a person, with little or no flexibility, and are so embedded in a person's daily routine activities that he or she hardly recognizes their existence. Men may hold on to their beliefs regarding what it means to be masculine and avoid anything feminine. These beliefs influence their behavior as men and their thoughts about men and women. Additionally, gender roles and stereotyping profoundly affect not only each individual in the family but also the relationship among individuals in the family, as well as the relationships between the family and the larger society.

The feminist perspective provides both men and women with a lens that focuses on knowledge and awareness to liberate them from the bondage of prescribed and well-established dysfunctional gender roles (Meth, 1990). Although not every problem that men bring to counseling is gender related, feminist counselors recognize that many of them bring along issues caused by rigid societal prescriptions that dictate how men should and should not act, think, and feel.

In this chapter, the issues and techniques of counseling men from a feminist family therapy perspective are offered. This discussion does not assume applicability to all men or women because such overgeneralization defeats several premises of the feminist approach. Counselors using feminist family therapy as their approach are advised that the issues are complex and solicit various kinds of responses from fellow practitioners, supervisors, supervisees, or clients. The core idea of this approach often elicits professional, ethical, and personal issues, especially when working with traditional men and women. It also challenges the status quo, that is, familiar ways of doing things. The approach is relatively new, and it is still evolving. It is attracting more attention from practitioners while, at the same time, as in any growing approach, having its own unexplored issues. Many of these unexplored issues occur around the intersection of race, ethnicity, and culture. The perspective offered in this chapter is culturally bound and applies mostly to White European men. Differences occur both within individuals in the dominant culture and between cultural groups.

Counseling Men: Issues

Counselors using a feminist family therapy approach must recognize the powerful impacts that gender socialization have on men. To seek counseling, men who are the products of such socialization must violate several principles of their beliefs of stereotypical "manhood." By seeking counseling services, the male client challenges the premises of a perception or belief of being a "real man," one who is supposedly self-reliant, invulnerable, and in control. Thus, seeking counseling in itself can be seen as requiring courage from the male client because counseling is an act that challenges the foundations of what is considered masculine. In counseling, "real men" who are preoccupied with knowing the rules and keeping score and who prefer rational, active solutions will face ambiguity and emotional talk, an antithesis to their concept of masculinity and a taunt to both client and counselor alike. These issues may be intensified when the therapist is female.

Zunker (1998) stipulated that special programs are needed to help men reevaluate their roles, beliefs, and values in all spheres of their lives, including their relationships with women in the home and workplace. Many men may have difficulty sharing family roles. Men, socially conditioned to play the role of a "king of the household," may have issues regarding the management and sharing of household tasks. This issue is becoming more prevalent with the increasing number of dual-career families. Increasingly, more men, especially those who are recently divorced, may now be forced to learn the balancing acts of juggling responsibilities of parenthood and managing a home and work.

The process of socialization is largely responsible for many powerful gender biases that men have, including a fear of femininity. These fears, in turn, influence the way men act, feel, and behave. Hence, men avoid any behavior or mannerisms construed to be feminine and put forth concentrated efforts to appear nonfeminine and, by default, masculine (Zunker, 1998). O'Neil (1982, as quoted in Zunker, 1998) stated that men's typical self-disclosure is restrictive because of the fear that their thoughts and actions might be associated with femininity. The conflicts, stress, and strain that men experience in living their stereotypical gender role can result in health problems. Masculine role conflicts have been found to be associated with psychological distress related to depression. Among the severe symptoms of distress are paranoia, psychoses, and obsessive–compulsive disorder (Good, Robertson, Fitzgerald, Stevens, & Bartels, 1996). Emotional expression and self-disclosure can be serious problems for men. Through gender role socialization, men may believe that expression of grief, pain, or weakness is perceived to be unmanly and therefore resist being open, honest, and expressive because such expressions are considered an open admission of vulnerability and loss of control. This restrictive emotionality may be a leading cause of poor interpersonal relationships between and among men, between men and women, and between men and children.

Stereotypical masculine traits such as competitiveness, independence, and self-reliance, if adopted and valued inappropriately, interfere with men's ability to learn to relax. Men's typical leisure activities that involve those values to the extreme are not conducive to relaxation. A typical social gathering could be spoiled and ruined when men try to outdo each other. A supposedly relaxed game of cards or checkers could turn into a fight. This is important because leisure is a source of need satisfaction, and the choice and control of leisure are important to self-esteem and holistic health (Herr & Cramer, 1996). Zunker (1998) stated that intense competition among men in the workplace might result in some men being very reluctant to be honest with their peers and having difficulties in developing interpersonal relationships. Thus, intense competition among men may be highly related to stressful work environments and work anxiety.

In their clinical experience working with men, Allen and Gordon (1990) saw their clients with very real problems revolving around fears of dependency, vulnerability, femininity, self-disclosure, and failure. These fears in turn threatened the men's gender identity, which underlay many of their clients' presenting problems. Thus, the problems and stresses men experienced when they entered counseling revolved around shifting images of masculinity, especially in the areas of autonomy, emotionality, and relationships. There appeared to be some resentment and sadness for some male clients because the privileges of being a man as dictated by the cultural socialization process did not lead them to their perceived rewards.

Men who believe and live up to stereotypical rigid masculine roles that emphasize separateness, independence, and control often experience emotional and physical trouble and perceive their life as "out of balance" (Allen & Gordon, 1990, p. 134). Many men grow up believing that relationships are the primary work of women. Men often rely on women to take responsibility for maintaining connection with other people in their lives. For example, women are expected to maintain contact with extended family on both sides and plan family rituals, celebrations, and social events with others. When the marriage or relationship breaks up, men often are left feeling bereft and lonely. As a result, men tend to lose many more connections than just the relationship with the wife or lover, leading them to experience stress and dysfunction. Typically, the greatest imbalance occurs between work and family. All too often, men are overly invested in their work at the expense of familial relationships.

Part of being "manly" is to deny and to dissociate from such natural human feelings as fear, sadness, and dependency. Logic and rational thought are valued as "masculine" traits, whereas so-called emotional responses, such as being fearful, compassionate, anxious, irrational, dependent, and indecisive, are designated as "feminine" characteristics and are thus to be avoided by men. The one emotion seemingly acceptable for men is anger. This restricted emotionality may be associated with violence, addictive behavior, fear of intimacy, communication and relationship problems with women, and difficulty in parenting. The internal lives of many men are manifested in communication problems with significant women in their lives. If these communication problems are to be resolved, men must learn how to recognize, own, and express their feelings.

Self-understanding and developing options for ways to change could be general goals for men in feminist family therapy. Feminist family therapy offers men opportunities that they normally do not allow themselves, such as expressing their emotions, admitting to their emotional needs, and confessing "weakness." Feminist family counseling also provides an opportunity for counselors to educate clients about the restrictiveness and potential destructiveness inherent in their beliefs about gender and to help them develop options from a wide range of life choices. Gender socialization is a central concern and is a part of therapy that must be addressed with all clients.

Counseling Men: Techniques

Two of the major principles of a feminist family therapy approach—the personal is political and counselor–client interactions are seen as egalitarian—guide counselors in delivering counseling services. "The personal is political" refers to the need to become aware of how people's lives are being influenced by societal expectations and roles, whereas the egalitarian relationship refers to counselors treating clients as equals and collaborating in the counseling process. Men who have been socialized to be providers of help may enter counseling with different expectations and thus provide counselors with unique challenges. It is not uncommon to find men seeking treatment because of external pressures or a forceful referral because of crisis in the family, at work, or with physical health. Such clients may bring considerable shame and hostility into the session, which are usually projected onto the counselor. Counselors often have a harder time gaining trust and commitment to the counseling process from men than from women. During the initial stage of counseling, in order not to turn clients off and not to reinforce their stereotypical notion that counseling is a "touchy-feely" exercise, counselors may want to use the "male" model of communication. The methods suggested by Allen and Gordon (1990) include defining the boundaries of counseling and giving clients some control over the process. Counselors could utilize strategies such as setting goals, using lists and diagrams, delineating tasks in sessions, and creating contracts to structure the counseling relationship. This is the time when counselors want to reframe clients' sense of desperation and failure for having to turn to professional counselors into one of strength and determination, facilitating clients' feelings that they are in control of their self-doubts. Next, counselors may want to normalize the client's immediate problems and assist him in appreciating the larger social context of his problem, allowing him to defuse some of his guilt and shame (Allen & Gordon, 1990).

When counseling men, Allen and Gordon (1990) begin by assessing the beliefs of the individual client, mainly to examine and appreciate the restrictive quality of his belief system. In dealing with men's restrictive self-disclosure, counselors are encouraged to use videotape presentations, role clarification exercises, feedback, group counseling, and peer-group interactions to illustrate unexpressive behaviors and to demonstrate the impact of unexpressive behaviors on interpersonal relationships (Zunker, 1998). Thus, working with male clients begins with the task of identifying the beliefs that they hold about masculinity, the sources of those beliefs in societal institutions and in the family of origin, and some of the potentially harmful results of those beliefs. Then, connection between those beliefs and the presenting problems must be made, while at the same time cautioning the client that those are freely chosen beliefs ("not carved in stone") and that they can be changed, should the client choose to do so.

To help men become comfortable with the therapeutic process, counselors are encouraged to be patient, nonthreatening, and nonjudgmental. Allen and Gordon (1990) stated that the "thinking through" process of counseling provides men the impetus and direction for change. They suggested that the counselor use reframing to explain the client's difficulties in a readily acceptable way by associating those difficulties with his detrimental set of beliefs about the meaning of manhood. Clients may begin to identify certain negative effects of male socialization, including a fear of experiencing some basic human qualities such as vulnerability, dependency, and the need for nurturing. Often, when men see how little choice they have had in generating their beliefs about masculinity, they react by questioning some of their lifelong premises and become able to imagine and accept different options.

Allen and Gordon (1990) help their clients understand the strong connection between their beliefs about gender and their problematic behaviors. They encourage their clients to change their "reality" about the meaning of masculinity to a more functional one. Facilitating this recognition also helps men to accept that their emotional needs are basic needs. Feminist family counselors continue to help male clients understand their needs for connectedness and ways to connect. This also helps clients understand the profound influences of their family of origin and find ways to differentiate themselves in healthy ways.

Counselors need to encourage men to get in touch with their deep sense of longing for relational connectedness as espoused by a feminist family therapy approach. This is an opportune time to assist the male client to connect with himself and his own feelings, thoughts, and knowledge. Human connection is a fundamental locus of psychological development, whereas disconnection is a basis of diminished self-esteem, energy, awareness, and disempowerment (Giblin & Chan, 1995). Usually, this process begins with counselors demonstrating and diagramming how men's lives are centered on performance and competition in the work area. This is followed with a discussion that focuses on how relationships are pushed to the periphery when work takes center stage.

Counselors can be effective in pointing out the irony of the situation in which male clients end up losing, through overzealousness at work, those very relationships that they had hoped to secure by hard work. Men can easily connect their ability to support a family to their efforts for recognition and achievement in the workplace. The awareness of this connection is an opportunity for feminist family counselors to stress that the solution becomes the problem when this motivation overshadows other aspects of life. This situation precludes men from the kind of connectedness to family, friends, and other pursuits that could enrich and support them. Feminist family counselors help clients realize that their lives are out of balance and out of control in many ways. One of the goals of a feminist family therapy approach is to facilitate men's understanding of interdependence and connectedness as positive values that anchor one's life. This adaptive balance is not achieved through passivity but is created through active choices made on the basis of developing self-knowledge, including an appreciation of present and past influences (Allen & Gordon, 1990).

Feminist family therapists may introduce a model of a balanced person, one who can participate fully and comfortably in relationships without fear of compromising or losing autonomy or being overwhelmed by closeness. This modeling sets the stage for counselors to challenge the vision of maleness as logical and unemotional. Feminist therapists can further challenge male clients with an idea that traditional men, because of gender role socialization, may use "logic" as a detour route to avoid their own fear of experiencing strong emotions. This avoidance of experiencing strong internalized emotions serves as an intellectual defensive response against normal, natural human feelings. With this understanding, male clients can be helped to see the negative aftermath of their emotional denial.

One of the most powerful and enduring influences in people's lives is the family in which they grew up. Revisiting family-of-origin issues is immensely valuable in helping men to rid themselves of emotional baggage around gender issues and relationships. When a client understands that unresolved emotional issues are often rooted in the family of origin and that these issues may impede his development of healthy and satisfying relationships throughout life, he also learns how the unresolved emotional issues from the past trigger automatic behavioral responses in the present. The main task a feminist family counselor is trying to achieve here is moving the client toward acceptance of his need for connectedness. Men often bury this need with a deep sense of grief, often masked by feelings of anger, indifference, or both. Often men are puzzled over finding themselves repeating behavior patterns they detested in their parents, especially their fathers. As these men identify the emotional triggers associated with earlier family relationships, they will begin to see how these triggers reappear and are reactivated in other relationships.

The Counselor

Feminist counselors understand the differences of growing up male or female in society. The profound results of gender role socialization compound the effects those differences have in terms of power, status, position, and privileges that a person enjoys within his or her family and in society in general (Goldenberg & Goldenberg, 2000). To provide effective counseling using a feminist family therapy approach with men, counselors are greatly challenged to examine and be aware of their own value system and the results of their own gender role socialization experiences. They recognize the impact of social, cultural, and political factors on their own lives. They accept the fact that some behaviors are or may be the reflection of internalized social norms or standards held by individuals. Furthermore, despite their training and experience, they recognize that they are neither immune from social influences nor able to readily free themselves from traditional gender roles that inadvertently lead them to view clients not as people but as male or female. Notice how easy it is to fall into a vicious cycle of accepting gender stereotypes as "truth" and to perpetuate gender biases in therapy.

Counselors, in their attempts to empower clients and reverse the present inherent disparity between the sexes, choose a feminist family therapy perspective in part because it emphasizes the collaborative nature of the counseling relationship that values equality, fairness, and joint effort. Feminist counselors typically encourage clients to examine traditional gender roles, make nonstereotypical life choices, develop equality in the assigning of tasks in their relationships, experience their power and strength, and become their own person (Thomas, 1977, as cited in DeVoe, 1990). Feminist counselors serve as role models and share their values openly and honestly in an attempt to answer clients' questions and explore any unexamined values or assumptions that they may hold.

To work effectively with men, the counselor must first comprehend the fact that most men are unaware of how little control they exercise in their lives (Meth, 1990). Emerging from and experiencing masculine gender role socialization processes, men are equally disadvantaged as women and thus suffer from family and society's sanctions of rigid and limited roles they can play. Men's roles are typically confined to a narrow range of being a provider (which is masculine) much to the exclusion of being a nurturer (which is feminine). These stereotypes, when internalized, limit clients' perceived alternatives or options. The feminist family therapist helps clients recognize and transcend those limitations of their own perceived alternatives. DeVoe (1990) stated that counselors must understand how political, economic, and social forces profoundly affect every person. Thus, counselors' awareness of the diverse and complex lives that people live and their commitment to social change may assist them in establishing the egalitarian, collaborative counseling relationship advocated by feminist family therapists. Recognizing how social context influences men's sense of manhood, feminist counselors use this context as a point of reference in their counseling practices with men (Meth, 1990). Arnold et al. (1995) advocated that counselors first must admit their own sexism and go beyond thinking about male and female as a dichotomy in their counseling practices and personal lives. Counseling relationships, much like other relationships that counselors experience, are shaped and influenced by various cultural patterns of thinking, feeling, and behaving.

Gender-related issues, in spite of their importance and pervasiveness in people's daily lives, still receive lukewarm acceptance in the training of counselors. As for professional development, Whipple (1996) stressed the importance of counselors continuing to educate themselves about feminist theory, to discuss gender issues with colleagues and supervisors, and to allow their personal experiences and their culture to inform their style of therapy.

Conclusion

Feminist family therapy approaches offer both male and female counselors alternative ways of addressing issues in helping clients, especially men. Feminist approaches that emphasize mutuality, collaborative relationships, respect for individuality and uniqueness, and multiplicity of perspective empower and benefit clients as well as counselors. This chapter described the concerns and benefits in counseling men using a feminist family therapy approach. Feminist family therapy is not gender specific and definitely not for women only.

References

Allen, J. A., & Gordon, S. (1990). Creating a framework for change. In R. L. Meth & R. S. Pasick (Eds.), *Men in therapy: The challenge of change* (pp. 131–151). New York: Guilford Press.

Arnold, M. S., Carlson, J., Collins, B. G., Collins, T. M., Gonzalez, T., Hayes, S., Hoffmann, F. J., Hutchins, M., Kjos, D., Lee, C., Lewis, J. A., & Vernon, A. (1995). Women and men interested in gender: Can we talk? *The Family Journal: Counseling and Therapy for Couples and Families, 3,* 4–10.

Costa, L., & Sorenson, J. (1993). Feminist family therapy: Ethical considerations for the clinician. *The Family Journal: Counseling and Therapy for Couples and Families, 1,* 17–24.

DeVoe, D. (1990). Feminist and nonsexist counseling: Implications for the male counselor. *Journal of Counseling and Development, 69,* 33–36.

Dupuy, P. J., Ritchie, M. H., & Cook, E. P. (1994). The inclusion of women's and gender issues in counselor education programs: A survey. *Counselor Education and Supervision, 33,* 238–248.

Elliot, J. M. (1999). Feminist theory. In D. Capuzzi & D. R. Gross (Eds.), *Counseling and psychotherapy: Theories and interventions* (2nd ed., pp. 203–229). Upper Saddle River, NJ: Merrill.

Giblin, P., & Chan, J. (1995). A feminist perspective. *The Family Journal: Counseling and Therapy for Couples and Families, 3,* 234–241.

Goldenberg, I., & Goldenberg, H. (2000). *Family therapy: An overview* (5th ed.). Belmont, CA: Brooks/Cole.

Good, G. E., Robertson, J. M. , Fitzgerald, L. F., Stevens, M., & Bartels, K. M. (1996). The relations between masculine role conflict and psychological distress in male university counseling center clients. *Journal of Counseling and Development, 75,* 45–49.

Herr, E. L., & Cramer, S. H. (1996). *Career guidance and counseling through the life span: Systematic approach* (5th ed.). New York: HarperCollins.

Hoffman, R. M. (1996). Gender: Issues of power and equity in counselor education programs. *Counselor Education and Supervision, 36,* 104–112.

Meth, R. L. (1990). The road to masculinity. In R. L. Meth & R. S. Pasick (Eds.), *Men in therapy: The challenge of change* (pp. 3–34). New York: Guilford Press.

Myers, D. G. (1999). *Social psychology* (6th ed.). Boston: McGraw-Hill College.

Stevens-Smith, P. (1995). Gender issues in counselor education: Current status and challenges. *Counselor Education and Supervision, 34,* 283–293.

Whipple, V. (1996). Developing an identity as a feminist family therapist: Implications for training. *Journal of Marital and Family Therapy, 22,* 381–396.

Worden, M., & Worden, B. D. (1998). *The gender dance in couple therapy.* Pacific Grove, CA: Brooks/Cole.

Zunker, V. G. (1998). *Career counseling: Applied concepts of life planning* (5th ed.). Pacific Grove, CA: Brooks/Cole.

■ ■ ■

FEMINIST FAMILY THERAPY WITH FAMILIES IN DIFFERENT STAGES OF THE LIFE CYCLE AND WITH DIFFERING CONCERNS

5

Adolescents and Families From a Feminist Family Therapy Perspective

Tovah Sands, PhD
Suni Petersen, PhD

Many of the families who begin counseling do so because of intense concern over one or more adolescent members of the family. Turmoil in the life of an adolescent is reflected in the family with whom the adolescent resides. The teenage years bring about tremendous change on every level, including biological, cognitive, and affective changes. Sharply increased awareness and responsiveness to one's sexual and gendered self play a large part in the adolescent experience. Heightened pressure from family members, peers, and the culture at large to conform to sex role socialization messages extracts a tremendous toll from adolescents.

In most cultures, the family is the social unit that expresses society's values, expectations, roles, and stereotypes. Families teach culturally approved gender roles by treating and responding to girls and boys differently, holding different expectations for them, and exerting different social pressures on them. In the household in which the father acts as the head of the family and the mother as the caretaker of the family, the family teaches children the stereotypes of men as leaders in society and women as nurturers and peacekeepers (Lips, 1993).

Parents may be uncertain of how to respond to the changes associated with puberty and may, as a result, reinforce or even increase conventional gender role stereotyped behaviors, values, and personal characteristics (Eccles & Bryan, 1994). Parents are often bewildered, overwhelmed, and at a loss for what to do, as they watch helplessly as their previously effective parenting strategies become useless while their teenage child spirals beyond their control. And if an adolescent member of the family has problems, life may become unbearable for the entire family.

Feminist Family Therapy With Adolescents

Feminist family therapy is a particularly appropriate treatment modality for counselors working with families with adolescents. Families with adolescents who enter counseling often have problems centered on a young woman's cries for connection, a notion that illustrates fundamental feminist principles of the ways in which social and political contexts shape female development and psychotherapy with young women (Tolman, 1994). Young women who feel conflicted and confused by the barrage of societal messages often try to cope by denying aspects of their own experiences, thoughts, feelings, and scholastic abilities (Gilligan, Rogers, & Tolman, 1991). Feminist therapy makes explicit the relationship of gender to the family, thus allowing the family to consider a wider range of perspectives, behaviors, and solutions to problems in an atmosphere less bound by rigid definitions of roles and identity (Wright & Fish, 1997).

Issues of abuse and neglect are of particular concern for feminists because of the structurally based powerlessness of young people. Traditional therapeutic approaches that minimize the influence of the situational variables or environmental stressors on families act in effect to maximize the responsibility of the individual to "fix" his or her situation. Children almost always lack the power or influence to change many aspects of their environment. Situational factors that must be considered include race, gender, class, ethnicity, religion, and sexual lifestyle (Conoley & Larson, 1995).

Each of the fundamental principles of feminist therapy matches in almost perfect symmetry with concerns that are key regarding adolescents. The feminist principle of "the personal is political" serves to normalize the ultrasensitivity to culture that most adolescents feel. As peers and the social environment become top priority in the minds of adolescents, feminist therapists emphasize the importance of the environment, the culture, and the context in the counseling process. With feminist therapy, adolescents are encouraged to seek authenticity and respect in relationships and to challenge false and abusive relationships (e.g., Sapsford, 1997).

The principle of egalitarian relationships is pivotal for feminist therapy and meets adolescents' keen desire to be "treated as adults." Feminist therapists use a number of strategies to meet this objective, including enacting collaborative and respectful relationships. Respect is crucial, as any parent knows, to gaining the trust and cooperation of a teenager.

Finally, the feminist principle of valuing the female perspective is applicable in counseling with all family members. This principle centers on the feminist therapist's focus on valuing connections and relatedness for both female and male family members. This principle is demonstrated by feminist family counselors when they educate the family about the developmental needs that young women have for relatedness and intimacy. Girls and women find it very important to establish and maintain interpersonal connections (Gilligan, 1991). Both connection and autonomy are essential for healthy female development, and the feminist therapist assists families toward becoming mutually interdependent (Mirkin, 1994).

In this chapter, we illustrate in two case studies the use of the feminist principles of the personal is political, egalitarianism, and valuing the female perspective. Each case study begins with a description of the adolescent and presenting problem followed by a brief explanation of several traditional family therapy approaches. In contrast, the conceptualization of the cases and the treatment are then discussed using feminist family therapy. We have chosen two of the most common presenting problems seen in our practices: drug use and ungovernability.

Drug Use as a Presenting Problem

Jasmine's tough-girl attitude almost preceded her through the door as she entered my office. A 16-year-old tall, lanky, African American young woman, Jasmine was referred to counseling by Juvenile Court after being caught in possession of marijuana. This was her third offense related to drugs and alcohol, and she was faced with the threat of a long-term juvenile detention program. She was alone on her first visit.

Jasmine was the older of two daughters and had a conflictual relationship with her sister. When she was 14 years old, her father left for work one morning and never returned. Jasmine's current connection with her father consisted of infrequent, irregular visits and intermittent child support. School records indicated she was "an underachieving, troublesome, belligerent student." Her truancy increased in the last 2 years, coinciding with her father's abandonment and her introduction to drugs. Jasmine regularly uses marijuana and alcohol and occasionally uses heroin. Her peer-group connections involve seeking and using drugs.

It took several calls to Jasmine's mother before she was able to get time off from her job to accompany Jasmine to her fourth session. Their household was chaotic. Engagement between Jasmine and her mother and sister was organized around fighting that consisted of verbal yelling matches. Jasmine's mother presented with the same "I don't need anyone" attitude as Jasmine, although she was admittedly overwhelmed and isolated. She remains angry and bitter since her husband left. She reported "trying everything" with Jasmine, which consisted of alternating between punitive, denigrating actions and seeking friendship with her daughter. Her attempts were met with rejection and retributive, verbally punitive remarks from Jasmine. Mother and daughter each demonstrated anger toward each other and suffered privately from guilt. Mom felt she needed to be competitive to survive on her job but was unaware that she fostered this competition in the home as well. She was very afraid of failing both with her daughters and her job. She focused more attention on the job because she felt "that's what is holding this family together" and because the guidelines for doing well on the job were clearer than those with her daughters.

Traditional family therapy approaches.

Traditional approaches grew out of a culture in which a patriarchal model was followed. As social consciousness developed, the role of the therapist and both the goals and process of therapy have been modified. Yet, they are nevertheless embedded in an epistemology that disavows the politics inherent in their process. Traditional transgenerational family therapists might focus on the family projection process in which the mother projected her anger and bitterness onto Jasmine, who incidentally resembled her father. They might work to increase Mom's differentiation from her ex-husband and Jasmine's differentiation from Mom. Jasmine would be helped to deal with her unresolved attachment to her father and the triangulated relationship with both parents through reducing her reactivity. The therapist would coach this family to get them started in the direction of detriangulation and differentiation. The therapist might also consider Jasmine's drug use as a triangulation between

Jasmine and her mother. While these treatments may have immediate appeal to Jasmine and her family (differentiation may seem to support their "I don't need anyone attitude," and coaching would provide a direction that Mom does not feel she has), they actually undermine the most basic need of the three female family members, that of connection. They also do not provide a contextual explanation that highlights their strengths.

Traditional structural family therapists would extricate Jasmine from the coalition with her mother against her father, strengthen the relationship with her sister, and clarify boundaries. Boundary issues between Jasmine and her mother consist of reactive and alternating rigidity and diffusion. Such a treatment modality destabilizes the system even further unless the mother's need for connection is addressed.

Behavioral family therapy would establish a contract with Jasmine related to her drug use, placing the responsibility on her. The therapists would identify the problem behavior in the family, such as the escalation of conflict and fulfillment of responsibilities; address the function of symptom behavior in the family; and find alternative behaviors to bring the family together using naturally occurring and therapist-recommended reinforcements.

Solution-focused family therapy would identify successful family interactions and attempts by Jasmine to refrain from drug use and fulfill her responsibility. It would emphasize the family's ability to find solutions. While such an approach may empower Jasmine and her mother, to some degree, such empowerment occurs in the absence of relational connection.

Narrative and constructivist approaches overlap with many of the principles of feminism. The narrative therapist would explore the family members' beliefs and meanings, would question how these beliefs came about within the context of the culture, and would examine how changes they have already begun might affect their lives. Narrative therapists may address issues of power and dominance in this exploration. A major difference between solution-focused, narrative, and constructivist therapies and feminist therapy is the role of the therapist. The former three approaches place the therapist in a "not knowing" position in which the family members serve as the experts. Feminist therapists, on the other hand, share political information with families and acknowledge their personal values.

Feminist family therapy.

Jasmine had been referred for counseling by Juvenile Court, making her the identified client. When Jasmine walked in for her first session, I told her that I had informed the Court and her mother that I would not accept this referral until Jasmine herself hired me. I let Jasmine know that if she felt during the first session that I was not a good fit for her needs, I would help her find a more appropriate counselor on the basis of her criteria. This was my first step in letting Jasmine know that she had control and power in some of her life choices from that moment forward.

Jasmine was both curious and angry. She did not want to be there. During the first session, I did most of the talking since Jasmine did not trust anyone. I let Jasmine know that I understood that being an African American female adolescent and growing up in the United States are not easy. Young Black women like Jasmine must deal with all the typical adolescent developmental hurdles, but they must do this in the context of a society that devalues Blacks and women.

Approaching Jasmine with the feminist use of self, I talked about my own ethnicity and race and drew parallels and contrasts. I defined my belief and commitment to create a healthy counseling relationship, acknowledging racial similarities and differences. I discussed her rights, clearly letting her know about limits of confidentiality. I thanked Jasmine for taking the risk that she had in coming to the first session and for letting me know she did not want to be there. In this way, I acknowledged her truths, her strength for speaking them, and her right to speak what she felt and believed and to be heard.

It took a while before the armor of defensiveness that Jasmine wore began to shed. Jasmine talked about her drug use as a natural response to how tough her life was. She graphically discussed the violence, anger, and hypocrisy she saw in her world. I listened, showed respect for her stories, and validated her experience by using the feminist strategy of power analysis to draw the connection between what Jasmine was experiencing and the culturewide power stereotypes that govern society.

As Jasmine slowly began to share more of herself in counseling, she talked about her anger and isolation, an obviously unpleasant experience for her. I validated these feelings, using the feminist strategy of gender analysis to draw the connection between Jasmine's experience and the ways in which gender stereotypes pervade the culture. I discussed the way in which male models of isolation and autonomy organize the vast majority of public schools, citing the manner in which classroom environments in middle and high school are less personal and more competitive—and less female friendly—than elementary schools (Sadker & Sadker, 1994).

I assisted Jasmine in gaining some important perspectives on her experiences of the past few years. Jasmine's dad left when she was 14 years old, an already hard year for Jasmine, who was entering high school. She was faced with the challenge of making new friends in a large, predominately White school with decreased opportunities to get close to the teachers. This is a difficult time for many young women, a time when adolescents are particularly concerned with peer relationships and may be in special need of close adult relationships outside of the home (Mason, Cauce, & Gonzales, 1997).

When Jasmine's mother joined Jasmine for her fourth session, I began by asking the mother what she thought was going on in the family. The mother related a story of weariness and being overwhelmed by working hard all day long, then coming home to more work. I again used the strategy of power analysis to explore the context of the family's life, reviewing the difficulties that single mothers face in U.S. society. The time and energy of single parents are more stretched than those of other working parents. They are more prone to guilt regarding their children than other working mothers because of their sole parental responsibility, and compared with married people, they are less supported in their own personal needs (Goodrich, Rampage, Ellman, & Halstead, 1988).

I assisted both mother and daughter in seeing the connection between their personal problems and the larger societal system. I related that the developmental processes that Jasmine was going through are shaped in part by broader societal conditions and events that impinge on the family. I gave the example of the ways in which economic strains can disrupt parenting. I used these strategies to forge a relationship of trust among Mom, Jasmine, and myself, knowing that when families are under threat or pressure to attend counseling, it can contribute to their resistance in approaching treatment. I reframed resistance to counseling as a healthy response to the racism, oppression, and discrimination that the family has faced.

Healing in this family started to begin as the family came to honor their own strengths and resources and those of their community. The family had been struggling in isolation, and each family member had been trying to cope, unsuccessfully, with isolation. I valued the female perspective by encouraging Mom to acknowledge the many things she did well for which she did not give herself credit. Mom admitted that she was financially independent, she had a successful career, and she was active in her church. Encouraged by this acknowledgment of her competence, Mom made a decision to invite Jasmine's sister to join them in counseling sessions.

With the entire family present, I used the opportunity to assist the family in recognizing their connection with other African American families. I demonstrated my knowledge of Black families by reiterating some of the key areas of strength shared by many Black families. For this family, these strengths included the bond with their extended family, adaptability of family roles, a strong religious orientation, and a firm belief in the value of education and the work ethic (Boyd-Franklin, 1989). I guided the family in an examination of each of these strengths, recounting incidents of economic hardship and racism that they had dealt with together. We discussed ways in which the extended family could be a viable support network in times of crisis, and the family promised to seek closer ties with their relatives. Mother and daughters discussed ways they could share household responsibilities in a flexible manner that would benefit the whole family. Mother and daughters discovered that they shared a common stance of toughness and struggle. I assisted the family in redirecting their individual struggles into a shared effort to solve problems and create a sense of power. By reducing their focus on struggle and toughness, the tendency toward escalating conflicts in their relationships with each other and with others in their lives also decreased.

While the focus of the counseling sessions had predominantly centered on family interactions, Mom had been making weekly reports regarding Jasmine's behavior. After several months of counseling, Jasmine's behavior had improved in some areas—Jasmine and her sister engaged in significantly fewer conflicts, for example—but her behavior remained unsatisfactory in other ways. The family agreed that Jasmine would next meet individually with me.

Individual sessions with Jasmine began with a discussion of her behavior at school. I validated Jasmine's identity as "one of those loud Black girls," sharing insights about adolescent female African Americans who make a commitment to be visible as culturally specific women (Fordham, 1993). Jasmine, as a "loud Black girl," was actively resisting the stereotype that White middle-class females are the American norm. While emphasizing the positive aspects of this strategy, I encouraged Jasmine to find ways in which she could refuse to conform to White standards of "good behavior" without actually enacting "bad behavior" by breaking school rules.

Jasmine's drug activity constituted a problem of use, not abuse. She reported an inconsistent pattern centering more on gaining peer acceptance than drug-seeking behavior. From the beginning, I focused on her need for acceptance and connection. As Jasmine began to resolve these issues, her drug use dropped significantly.

Traditional approaches to substance abuse treatment are frequently ineffective for women because virtually all are designed for men and they fail to incorporate interventions that address the cultural, environmental, and societal contexts of women's lives (Uziel-Miller, Lyons, Kissiel, & Love, 1998; Walitzer & Connors, 1997).

The family came to a few more sessions together before terminating their counseling. During this time, I was able to introduce specific strategies to help reduce family conflict, such as communication skills, assertiveness training, and decision-making skills. The family practiced by role playing some of their daily conflicts in session. I taught the family ways to release anger that were healthy and beneficial.

Jasmine's mother contacted the youth group at her church and discovered that there was a church group that worked with families; she began attending those meetings. She contacted the school to find a tutor for Jasmine to help her improve her grades. The mother was encouraged to find positive role models for her daughters who would provide examples of African American women in successful careers.

During the 4 months that Jasmine met with me, her stance as a tough girl softened appreciably, taking shape not as an aggressive but as an increasingly assertive young woman. Although she did not resolve all her presenting problems, her behavior slowly changed for the positive: Her use of marijuana and alcohol decreased, and she had stopped all use of heroin. Her behavior at school was better, and she particularly thrived on the relationships with successful Black women in the community that her mother had initiated. I believe that the use of feminist counseling with close attention to racial and cultural issues was especially effective in working with Jasmine and her family.

Ungovernability as a Presenting Problem

It was Sonia's ungovernability that drew her family into the counseling services provided free of charge by the county's public schools. The intelligent and sociable bilingual first-generation Puerto Rican household consisted of Mom, Dad, Sonia, and her two siblings, Ricky and Gabriel. Ricky was 18, a school dropout, and unemployed. Gabriel was 8 and the delight of both parents. The family had moved to the mainland United States from Puerto Rico when Sonia, now 14, was 6 years of age.

Mom, Dad, and Sonia came together to the first counseling session. Appearing both reticent and anxious to get the story out, Mom quickly began the session by passionately relating that Sonia was really "a good girl," but her behavior had been getting so bad lately that they really did not know where else to turn. Dad said that he felt that Sonia was hanging out with the wrong kids, which led to getting in trouble at school for disruptive behavior, tardiness, and declining grades. Sonia and her mother were engaged in a long-term intense relationship that alternated between "best of friends" and a power struggle. Sonia was also close to her father. Two years prior to our counseling, Dad contracted an illness and became wheelchair bound.

Although Dad continued in his job, the family suffered severe financial hardship because of high medical bills and frequent absenteeism. Although Mom was capable of working, she sabotaged her success on the job by claiming her husband's illness as a reason for "not being able to cope" at work. All of these family members were talkative, intelligent, outgoing, and emotionally volatile. They had an extreme need to be a self-sufficient model family in the eyes of the community. They all presented a facade of independence that hid their intense dependency. Yet each time a crisis erupted, Dad, who suffered from disease-related fatigue, was drawn into the family to provide financial support or to discipline Sonia to support Mom.

Traditional family therapy approaches.

Traditional approaches that do not focus on the context or consider it irrelevant might see Sonia's father's illness as the triggering event that destabilized the system, knowing that illness coincided with a stress point in the life cycle of the family (Figley & McCubbin, 1983). Illness is an event that frequently draws families together because the need increases the unifying centripetal forces in the family at a time when, developmentally, centrifugal forces are at their height in raising adolescents (Carter & McGoldrick, 1980). For this family to function, they must achieve the unique and precarious balance of maintaining connections within the family and encouraging the assumption of nontraditional roles (Mom working and both children contributing in ways not normally prescribed in adolescence) while allowing for development to occur.

A traditional structural approach would separate the sibling subsystem from the parental subsystem. Because Mom's dependency was the most evident, the therapist would have interpreted that as a factor holding her elder son back, demanding friendship from her daughter, and sabotaging her work efforts. Two factors would gain therapeutic attention: first, the family's need to look "perfect" that prevented them from soliciting assistance from the larger community; second, their need for connection particularly when faced with adversity. Traditional family therapies would validate the need for support, and the family would be encouraged to seek assistance from outside groups or institutions. When viewed from this deficit model, the family's strengths may go unrecognized and unappreciated, further distancing the family from its resources.

The family has adapted to the father's illness by organizing their relationship in reaction to the illness. By conceptualizing the illness as a trigger, the traditional therapist would maintain this view of illness as the organizing feature. A traditional therapist may use role theory to explain the disruption of the "normal" family life cycle. The medical literature is replete with studies identifying the role changes required when illness strikes, the flexibility needed to change roles, and the poor effects on the family if role change cannot occur.

The fear of death was directing this family's organization. Whenever the family compensated adequately for Dad's limitations, Dad felt helpless and became seriously depressed, a condition that, in fact, exacerbated his illness. And although the mother acted in ways to assure her husband's place in the family, she withdrew emotionally because she was secretly preparing herself for his death. This may lead the traditional family therapist to work on anticipatory grief and discuss the intergenerational pattern of grieving within the extended family as an indicator of this family's model. Encouraging the expression of grief usually involves affective processes. However, this family did not lack in emotional expression; in fact, they saw their volatility as a problem.

The strategic approaches would focus on the problem-maintaining sequences and in doing so take a very directive stance, reframing the problem to increase the likelihood of compliance with their directives. The strategic technique of prescribing the symptom, Sonia's defiance, and acting out might escalate the distance between Sonia and her family, encouraging their view of her being the identified patient. Neutrality and therapist distance further enhance the hierarchy that adds to the cultural divide between the therapist and the Hispanic client family. From this perspective, all behaviors are seen as emanating from and within the family system with no regard to the cultural context.

Feminist family therapy.

The family's immediate crisis began 2 years ago when Dad became ill, bringing the unspoken fear of death into daily life. A trau-

matic situation in itself, the experience for this family was strained
even more by poverty and the differing rates of acculturation that
family members were experiencing. There was much in this family
that needed attention, but one of my first concerns was asking the
family to explain the cultural context in which these problems were
occurring. For example, I asked the family to explain how families
in Puerto Rico would deal with the problem of a daughter who dis-
obeys her parents and does poorly in school. By focusing initially
on the concern that the parents identified as the presenting problem, I was initiating a collaborative relationship with the family,
while simultaneously honoring the Hispanic tradition of *respecto*,
respect for authority, especially for those who are older (Marin &
Marin, 1991). This is an important way of establishing trust with
the family, particularly if the counselor is not also Hispanic. Dad
began by stating that in Puerto Rico bad girls are kept at home and
dealt with strictly by the family. I echoed their reticence to turn to
counseling and began the critical task of making the counseling
setting a safe environment for trust to develop. I used the feminist
strategy of demystifying the counseling process by explaining my
approach to counseling and by giving the family information such
as the policies of the agency and limits to confidentiality. I validated the family's willingness to share their story, acknowledging
the risk each of them took by entering a new place and facing a
new person to trust. I also inquired about the family's strengths.
Such inquiry has been demonstrated to change the perspective of
the therapist (Rafuls & Moon, 1996) toward viewing the family more
positively.

As counseling proceeded, it became apparent that much of the
conflict between Sonia and her family could be traced to their differing rates of acculturation. As the parents tried to maintain the
cultural values and customs of their homeland, their children had
greater exposure to the norms of the new culture through school
and friendships. With my encouragement, Sonia began to tell her
parents of her struggle to balance connections with two cultures.
This revelation and the perspective it brought to the family became
a valuable tool in reframing the conflictual relationships the family
was experiencing.

I used the strategy of gender role analysis as we discussed the
developmental struggle that Sonia, a Puerto Rican adolescent female, was encountering. The link between Sonia's dilemma and the
culture's gender stereotypes and power relations was important for
the family to understand as they began to examine the struggle
between Sonia and her mother. It was important that the family

recognized that Sonia was becoming an adolescent in a majority Anglo neighborhood and school, and Anglo peer approval was excruciatingly important to her. Conflict arose in the family when Sonia tried to win approval from her peers by adopting many of their values, and her mother interpreted these behaviors as turning against the family and its values and as misbehaving and being disrespectful. Cultural precepts about becoming a woman are often promoted most strongly by the mother (Petersen, 2000). Sonia felt as if she was in a terrible bind of having to choose between her family and her friends. Faced with an unbearable choice, she let her confusion and anger out at her mother.

Sonia's mother, staying at home, was angry with her daughter for her new American ways and for the disrespect she experienced. Yet, at the same time, she felt dependent on her daughter to navigate the new culture, a role she would not ask of the male members in the family. For Sonia, a painfully self-conscious adolescent, having a stay-at-home Mom who made no attempt to assimilate into the mainstream culture became a source of great embarrassment.

Gender role analysis revealed that the family had strict gender and familial role expectations that they expected Sonia to fill. Asking the family to explain the Hispanic norms of femininity, the counselor learned about *familialismo*, a strong family bond that included the importance of obedience and passivity on the part of daughters (Marin & Marin, 1991). Sonia, as the only daughter, was expected to become even more involved with household tasks, yet this was in direct conflict with what she saw in the families of her new peers. Mom and Dad did not ask her brothers to assist because they believed that household chores were "woman's work." Through gender role analysis, the family began to recognize that many factors, including the children's developmental stressors, strict gender role expectations, and differing rates of acculturation, had contributed to the making of the family crisis when Dad became ill.

Meeting separately with the parents, I used the feminist strategy of power analysis to enable Mom and Dad to see the link between the personal problems in their marriage and those of culturewide power relations between the dominant culture in the United States and immigrant minorities. They began to understand that everyone in the family had been tremendously affected by the move to the mainland, and each was privately shocked by their acquired status as an ethnic minority in the United States. In the safety of the counseling environment, the parents were able to verbalize and deal with feelings of anger, guilt, and self-degradation imposed by their immigrant status.

Gender role analysis enabled the parents to understand that their enactment of traditional gender roles was contributing to the financial, emotional, and physical detriment of the family since their move to the mainland. I emphasized the good intentions of the parents by pointing out, for example, that Mom was trying to teach her daughter how to be a "good woman" by Puerto Rican terms. However, by endorsing a stereotypical feminine role, the parents were teaching their daughter to "acculturate" to an oppressive role.

I also brought up the issue of power dynamics inherent in the parents' relationship. By verbalizing this covert issue, the parents began to see that their reluctance for Mom to work outside the home not only hurt the family's financial standing but also sent a powerful message to Sonia. At an age when Sonia was immensely impressionable about her future as a woman, her parents' actions said in effect that she did not need to be successful in school or work but that a "good woman" would marry a man who would support her financially.

I worked with the parents to design an intervention that emphasized the importance of both parents working together to resolve additional family conflicts, such as their uneasiness about Ricky's unemployment and dropout status. We tried to work out a strategy that would respect the position of the mother as the family's expert on child rearing and would also speak to the benefits that Dad would experience for increasing his involvement in the day-to-day functioning of the family. The parents agreed that they would work together to enforce the house rules for Sonia, Ricky, and Gabriel. Through counseling, they discovered that the profound and deep love that they both shared for their children created a unity that enabled them to work through the upheavals inherent in their shifting family roles and relationships. The counseling sessions became an empowering experience for Mom, who began to recognize the tremendous influence she did have on her daughter. With her husband's and my support, she agreed to look for work.

I then met with Sonia individually. Sonia's behavior had improved since her family had been in counseling; however, much work remained. It became clear that Sonia was having a deep identity struggle. Because her thoughts and feelings often differed from the conventions of Hispanic culture, Sonia was confused and saddened at the feeling that she could not still think of herself or be thought of by her parents as a "good Spanish daughter." I helped Sonia to understand that she was experiencing a crisis of connection. She was struggling to know, to speak about, and to act on her own thoughts and feelings, while at the same time trying to stay connected to her peers, her family, and her identity as a Hispanic girl. Sonia spoke about the deep anxiety and frustration she experienced in these relationships.

Sonia and I worked to develop a definition of biculturality that was comfortable for her. We developed a framework in which the conflicts between parents and children were framed as a generational struggle in response to the two different cultures coming together in the family. In this way, conflict was framed in cultural terms rather than in terms of "disobedient daughter" and "unreasonable" parents. Sonia later shared this with her family, pointing out the positive values from each culture that she incorporated into her bicultural framework. This also led to an important development in counseling for Sonia: a more positive way to experience her mother. As both mother and daughter changed, Sonia slowly came to take pride in her mother's skills as a survivor, an explorer, a tradition breaker, and a tradition keeper.

Sonia and I focused on her grades and the pull of her "wrong crowd" of friends. I encouraged Sonia to use journal writing as an avenue to express her feelings openly, as well as to chronicle her transitions through school and her interactions with peers and family members. A bright and verbal girl, she adopted this idea readily. Sonia also suffered from not feeling accepted by and different from her peers. An important component of our counseling together was for me to guide her toward the understanding that she does not need to be accepted and loved by everyone. We talked about what she wanted in a romantic relationship, with emphasis on redefining gender roles.

Other issues of concern with Sonia included lack of career planning. I suggested books for Sonia to read that depicted girls and women in positive roles. We discussed academic and career goals, including values and the relevance of math and science classes. I introduced Sonia to women who were successful in fields in which she had shown interest and abilities. Dad contacted the school and found a tutor for several subjects.

Fear of death had immobilized this family and trapped them in their rigid roles. Because Mom had remained true to her cultural definition of wife and mother, she needed to acquire the skills to negotiate the new world in which they lived. The empowerment that Mom experienced in counseling reduced her fear and opened the door to new learning. Dad, who was initially threatened by his own growing inability to care for his family, knew their survival was no longer threatened. When the family came together again, they were finally ready to discuss their fear of death without being overwhelmed about this very painful but inescapable family issue.

Few issues in counseling generate as much grief as the anticipated death of a family member, and this family was no exception. Their approach to death was honest and courageous, and through their newly discovered strength as a family, they confronted the inevitable together. As a consequence of their work in feminist family counseling, this family was able to share their remaining time together as a much more supportive, egalitarian, and caring family.

Conclusion

Through the lives of Jasmine and Sonia, feminist treatment strategies were demonstrated. With Jasmine's family, the need for connection, an analysis of the effects of race and gender, and the lack of support provided by the culture for single parents were emphasized. With Sonia's family, the intersection of acculturation and development, as well as gender stereotypes, was explored.

Any therapy that does not work within the redefinition of healthy development for adolescent girls does not promote true growth and healing. Traditional treatments that are built on a foundation of autonomy set an impossible goal for the adolescent girl—that is, growing in one's independence and emotional–physical self-sufficiency while not only preempting the connections she needs to do so but also doing so within a culture that consistently and systematically erects obstacles to the achievement of her goals. Disregarding this fact, as most traditional approaches do, constitutes maintaining the political status quo, leaving these young women in a continuing state of vulnerability. Isn't that antitherapeutic?

References

Boyd-Franklin, N. (1989). Five key factors in the treatment of Black families. *Journal of Psychotherapy and the Family, 6*(1–2), 53–69.
Carter, E. A., & McGoldrick, M. (1980). *The family life cycle: A framework for family therapy.* New York: Gardner Press.
Conoley, J. C., & Larson, P. (1995). Conflicts in care: Early years of the lifespan. In E. J. Rave & C. C. Larsen (Eds.), *Ethical decision making in therapy: Feminist perspectives* (pp. 202–222). New York: Guilford Press.

Eccles, J., & Bryan, J. (1994). Adolescence: Critical crossroad in the path of gender-role development. In M. R. Stevenson (Ed.), *Gender roles through the life span: A multidisciplinary perspective* (pp. 111–147). Muncie, IN: Ball State University.

Figley, C. R., & McCubbin, H. I. (1983). *Stress and the family: Vol. II. Coping with catastrophe.* New York: Brunner/Mazel.

Fordham, S. (1993). "Those loud Black girls": (Black) women, silence, and gender "passing" in the academy. *Anthropology and Education Quarterly, 24*(1), 3–32.

Gilligan, C. (1991). Women's psychological development: Implications for psychocounseling. In C. Gilligan, A. G. Rogers, & D. L. Tolman (Eds.), *Women, girls and psychocounseling: Reframing resistance* (pp. 5–32). New York: Haworth Press.

Gilligan, C., Rogers, A. G., & Tolman, D. L. (1991). Introduction to women, girls and psychotherapy: Reframing resistance. *Women and Therapy, 11*(3–4), 1–3.

Goodrich, T. J., Rampage, C., Ellman, B., & Halstead, K. (1988). *Feminist family therapy: A casebook.* New York: Norton.

Lips, H. M. (1993). *Sex and gender: An introduction* (2nd ed.). Mountain View, CA: Mayfield.

Marin, G., & Marin, B. (1991). *Research with Hispanic populations.* Newbury Park, CA: Sage.

Mason, C. A., Cauce, A. M., & Gonzales, N. (1997). Parents and peers in the lives of African-American adolescents: An interactive approach to the study of problem behavior. In R. D. Taylor & M. C. Wang (Eds.), *Social and emotional adjustment and family relations in ethnic minority families* (pp. 85–98). Mahwah, NJ: Erlbaum.

Mirkin, M. (1994). Female adolescence revisited: Understanding girls in their sociocultural context. In M. Mirkin (Ed.), *Women in context: Toward a feminist reconstruction of psychotherapy* (pp. 77–95). New York: Guilford Press.

Petersen, S. (2000). Multicultural perspective on middle-class women's identity development. *Journal of Counseling and Development, 78,* 63–71.

Rafuls, S. E., & Moon, S. (1996). Grounded theory methodology in family therapy research. In D. M. Sprenkle & S. M. Moon (Eds.), *Research methods in family therapy* (pp. 64–80). New York: Guilford Press.

Sadker, M., & Sadker, D. (1994). *Failing at fairness: How America's schools cheat girls.* New York: Scribner's.

Sapsford, L. (1997). Strengthening voices: A soulful approach to working with adolescent girls. *Women and Therapy, 20*(2), 75–87.

Tolman, D. (1994). Listening for crises of connection: Some implications of research with adolescent girls for feminist psychotherapy. *Women and Therapy, 15*(2), 85–100.

Uziel-Miller, N. D., Lyons, J. S., Kissiel, C., & Love, S. (1998). Treatment needs and initial outcomes of a residential recovery program for African-American women and their children. *American Journal on Addictions, 7*(1), 43–50.

Walitzer, K. S., & Connors, G. J. (1997). Gender and treatment of alcohol-related problems. In R. W. Wilsnack & S. C. Wilsnack (Eds.), *Gender and alcohol: Individual and social perspectives* (pp. 445–461). New Brunswick, NJ: Rutgers Center of Alcohol Studies.

Wright, C. I., & Fish, L. S. (1997). Feminist family therapy: The battle against subtle sexism. In N. V. Benokraitis (Ed.), *Subtle sexism: Current practice and prospects for change* (pp. 201–215). Thousand Oaks, CA: Sage.

6

Feminist Family Therapy With the Elderly

A. Renee Staton, PhD

Family therapists working from a feminist perspective often face a daunting task: identifying and confronting gender and other stereotypes that perpetuate oppressive and patriarchal systems. Although general awareness of and dissatisfaction with gender-based inequity appear to be growing, Western societies continue to afford men, especially young, White, Protestant, heterosexual men, with a different power than what they afford women (Lorde, 1995; McIntosh, 1995). Add to this the fact that the notion of family is socially constructed (Anderson, 1995; Goodrich, Rampage, Ellman, & Halstead, 1988; Monk, 1997) and based on modernist views of gender, and the result is a complex system in which ideas about men, women, mother, and father become reified. Roles and rituals have the patina of truth, and challenging that truth, as many feminist therapists do, may appear foolish and threatening. After all, roles help people make sense of their world by providing them with a set of expectations. However, "people created [roles], and sometimes other people need to re-create or even discard them" (Anderson, 1995, p. 115). Re-creating, and sometimes discarding, roles is a relatively common goal of most effective therapies, including feminist family therapy (Goodrich et al., 1988).

This goal is especially important when working with the elderly family. Although theorists and researchers have disagreed as to whether counseling elderly clients is fundamentally different from counseling younger clients (Myers, 1995), therapists working with elderly families face several distinct issues. First, ageism and its attendant stereotypes can and do interfere with the provision of mental health services to elderly clients (Hashimi, 1991; Wimmers, 1983). Counselors may believe that the elderly have less capacity for change compared with younger clients. As a result, counselors' expectations may be lowered and their efforts decreased. Furthermore, the current societal trend of defining vitality and worth as equivalent to youth and beauty may negatively affect counselors' personal opinions of their elderly clients' dignity and appeal (Hendricks & Leedham, 1991; Poggi & Berland, 1985).

These stereotypical views also affect the elderly client. In many ways, the elderly in U.S. society constitute an oppressed population, because societal leadership and social organization rest on a power base that does not necessarily include the concerns of the elderly. Frequently, however, people learn to "accept as legitimate [the] conditions that lead to their own exploitation" (Hendricks & Leedham, 1991, p. 15). This type of hegemony may result in internalized oppression for aged populations, as evidenced by some elderly people who doubt their own agency and worth. Thus, ageism and its effects are likely to influence counseling efforts with elderly clients.

An additional concern for counselors is the fact that elderly clients' views of themselves are greatly influenced by their generational context. Elderly family members' gender roles, intergenerational patterns, and worldviews were formed in a more conservative and restrictive time. Although some families transcend societal expectation, traditional attitudes and beliefs have naturally had more time to become reinforced and habitual for the elderly family. In addition, roles that are accepted and understood, even those that are essentially constraining, may be reassuring for elderly clients who increasingly feel they are losing control over their life and family. The stress resulting from loss of relatives and friends, increased isolation, decreased mobility, and financial dependence may increase the desire on the part of elderly family members to cling tenaciously to rigid roles that are comforting in their familiarity.

Finally, from a purely pragmatic standpoint, the elderly are often underserved or poorly served by mental health professionals (Hashimi, 1991; Myers, 1995). This unfortunate trend is due in part to the difficulties inherent in providing appropriate mental health services to elderly clients who may have ambulatory problems or inadequate access to transportation. The frequent use of a medical model and its emphasis on physiological symptoms and pathology when treating the elderly may also prevent therapists from adopting a more holistic and contextual view of the family and their concerns (Edinburg, 1985; Rathbone-McCuan, 1991). In addition, some therapists' negative reactions to the elderly and many elderly people's negative expectations of counseling (Kunkel & Williams, 1991) combine to create what appear to be formidable obstacles to effective and sensitive provision of mental health services for the elderly family.

Benefits of Feminist Family Therapy

Fortunately, the practice of family therapy in general, and feminist family therapy in particular, incorporates several core tenets that allow therapists to address these challenges while providing mental health care that liberates and empowers the elderly client. According to Edinburg (1985), family therapy is especially appropriate for the elderly because family therapists tend to explore the functional rather than to emphasize the pathological. This view of the family enables the therapist to honor the adaptive nature of clients' distress as a natural reaction to the aging process and its attendant stressors. The addition of a feminist perspective to family therapy ensures that the concerns of elderly family members are examined within the context of a series of systems that habitually reinforce restrictive and oppressive gender stereotypes. Thus, the therapist's understanding of the family's concerns is broadened.

Family therapists also focus on support systems (Edinburg, 1985), which tend to be a crucial consideration in the life of elderly clients. Examining the elderly family's support systems through a feminist lens increases the likelihood that traditional gender patterns of caregiving, family involvement, and general expectations of family members are identified and addressed. A feminist approach to family therapy also enables the therapist to expand and perhaps replace traditional definitions of support systems. By critically examining and challenging current definitions of "family," for instance, feminist family therapists increase their ability to accept the family as it is, rather than as it "should be" according to societal standards. The reality for many elderly families is a reliance on neighbors, friends, and volunteers, all of whom may become "family" to the elderly. A feminist approach to family therapy recognizes and accepts this reality.

Finally, family therapy allows for an exploration of the interactional patterns between family members, including the underlying dynamics and the role of power in these patterns (Edinburg, 1985). Feminist family therapy, with its emphasis on addressing and correcting the oppressive stereotypes embedded in relationships (Goodrich et al., 1988; Walters, Carter, Papp, & Silverstein, 1988), is therefore an especially appropriate modality for intervening with the elderly family. These families have intergenerational communication patterns that have often become extremely intricate over time, thereby demanding a critical analysis that incorporates an awareness of societal influences on individual family members.

A feminist approach to family work therefore offers a framework for providing effective, empathic therapy for the elderly. By consistently exploring the influence of gender roles and gender stereotypes on the family, feminist therapists have the opportunity to empower family members by revealing new possibilities, generating hope, and effecting positive change both within and beyond the family system. A case study is included that illustrates the unique demands, as well as opportunities, involved in family therapy with elderly clients.

The Carson Family

I first met Rose Carson, the matriarch of the Carson family, after the agency for which I was working received a frantic call from her neighbor, Carolyn. During the phone call, Carolyn reported that she feared Rose was severely depressed and receiving insufficient care from her family. Rose had limited access to transportation and was struggling with mobility because of complications related to a diabetic condition, so I made arrangements to visit her in her home.

Although home visits are often considered a breach of the traditional boundaries of many types of therapy, in this case the visit was considered not only appropriate but also necessary. After talking with a medical social worker involved in this case, it became evident that the effort involved in obtaining transportation to the office would prevent Rose from seeking therapy. Furthermore, I viewed the home visit as an opportunity to assess Rose's living conditions as well as increase the likelihood that I could involve her family in therapy.

When I first met with Rose, she was alone. She appeared frail and was occasionally distraught as she told me about her background and history. Rose was a 79-year-old woman who had been widowed for over 40 years. She had reared and been the primary caretaker for seven children, four of whom were still living: Roy, age 54; Joan, age 49; Janice, age 47; and William, age 45. Rose also reported having numerous—too numerous to count, she said—grandchildren, great-grandchildren, nieces, and nephews.

According to Rose, she was extremely depressed because she felt her children had deserted her. This sense of desertion had become apparent to Rose when she was hospitalized for treatment of a diabetes-related condition and none of her family called or came to visit her. Her isolation was especially difficult for Rose now because she had been accustomed to her son William living with her. William had lived with Rose until very recently but had moved out after the two had argued about his relationship with his girlfriend. Since being admitted to and then released from the hospital, Rose had not spoken to William. Once, though, William had evidently asked a neighbor to tell Rose "hello." Roy, Rose's other son, also communicated with Rose through neighbors. Roy was an alcoholic and had been told by Rose not to visit unless he was sober. He had not visited in months. Rose's daughters, Joan and Janice, both lived out of state. Although they had been informed that Rose had been ill, Rose reported that neither one of her daughters had called or written.

While relating her history, Rose vacillated between holding herself accountable for the condition of the family and then blaming her children for being selfish and cruel. Her affect and presence likewise shifted from tearful and despondent when she was blaming herself to animated and angry when she was blaming her children. She said several times that she knew life had been difficult for her children. When her children were young, Rose and her husband had had a fairly volatile relationship. Her husband eventually moved out of the house. Although the two never divorced, they had a much better relationship after he moved out, in spite of, or perhaps because of, the fact that his involvement in the family was minimal.

As she reflected back on this time, Rose described herself as being both mother and father to her children, explaining that she had to "be tough" sometimes when the children were growing up. Being the sole caretaker for seven children often required so much of her physical energy that she felt she had little else to give. Rose suggested that perhaps if she had been nicer, the children would treat her better now. Soon after making such a statement, however, Rose would quickly remind herself of how tirelessly she had worked to support and care for her children, recalling instances of sacrifice when she had provided the family with moments of joy. What more could she have done?

I was somewhat pleased to see Rose grow angry as she described her children's role in the current situation, in part because her anger provided the energy she would need to combat her depression, but also because the anger revealed her awareness of the injustice of her situation. At times, Rose seemed to become aware of the fact that her children's behavior could not always be traced back to her treatment of them during their childhood. Occasionally she would refer to them as adults who, she believed, should have some sense of responsibility and sensitivity to her current situation. She was alone and ill and wanted to know that her family cared for her. That did not seem too much to ask. Frequently, though, this line of reasoning would lead Rose back to blaming herself for the fact that her children did not seem to have that sense of responsibility and sensitivity she expected. She would then lose the fire of her wounded anger, and her cloud of despair would return.

During the initial session, three factors emerged that seemed particularly relevant from a feminist point of view. First, part of Rose's suffering seemed related to her acceptance of society's myths regarding motherhood as the ultimate institution of responsibility. In her eyes, her adult children's behaviors were dictated by Rose's own behavior as a mother 40-plus years ago. She had internalized the oppression of mother-blaming and turned it on herself with a vengeance.

Second, when Rose stated that perhaps if she had been "nicer" as a mother her children would treat her better now, she revealed that she had accepted prevailing gender stereotypes regarding the characteristics of the "perfect mother"—one who is always patient, kind, and warm toward her children. It is interesting to note that Rose's communication style was direct and assertive. I suspected that when Rose compared herself with societal images of the perfect mother, especially those images of the 1940s and 1950s when Rose herself was a young mother, she felt she had been insufficient. In an ironic twist, Rose exhibited many of the personality characteristics that our society prizes in men but despises in women.

Third, the fact that Rose was the primary breadwinner and caretaker of the family was itself a violation of the traditional model of the family. Even today, single-parent families are often portrayed as the true root of all societal problems, so I imagined that during Rose's time as a young mother she had felt fairly alone and that she and her children may have felt stigmatized by their family arrangement. This assumption was based on Rose's frequent attempts to defend her mothering behavior.

The information I gathered in the first session therefore suggested that Rose was indeed depressed and that this depression was related primarily to situations arising within her family. Although Rose's deteriorating physical condition, along with the accompanying decrease in mobility, undoubtedly contributed to her sense of despair, the content of our session focused primarily on her dissatisfaction with her life in connection with her family. With these ideas in mind, and with the desire to ensure that Rose received the in-home care she needed, I asked to meet with Rose again in the company of her family members. Rose expressed doubt that any of her children would attend a session with me. Her two sons were difficult to reach. Roy had no phone, and William moved from one friend's home to another since he had moved out of Rose's apartment. Eventually, Rose promised to enlist her neighbors' help in contacting at least her son William and his son Michael.

I visited Rose again the next week and again found her alone. Carolyn, Rose's neighbor, had notified both William and Michael of my desire to meet with them, but neither one had come to Rose's apartment for the session. Rose presented in much the same manner as before, describing William and Michael's failure to attend the session as further evidence of the hopelessness of her family situation. Rose described herself as being in a prison, waiting for her children to come and visit her and feeling locked away from her friends and neighbors, whom she believed treated her much better than her children ever had.

I had initially believed that Rose stayed alone in her apartment because she had difficulty walking to her neighbors. At the second session, Rose told me that walking to her neighbors' homes was not difficult for her at all. In actuality, she stayed home for two reasons. First, if her children came to visit she wanted to be home; second, she needed to be home to receive the hot meals that were delivered to her by a volunteer organization. Rose explained that she enjoyed cooking and was still able to do so, but she found cooking for one person to be difficult and boring. If given a choice, she explained, she would spend the days at her friend Carolyn's house. At Carolyn's house people came in and out, children came by after school, there was plenty of company, and there were numerous jobs to do. As Rose described Carolyn's house, she smiled for the first time.

The next week I arrived at Rose's apartment and was pleased to see a young man with her. Michael, her grandson, had moved in with Rose, but he was unwilling to participate in therapy. He was polite but firm in his insistence that he not be involved. He indicated that he had moved in with Rose at the request of his father, William. William had heard that his mother was depressed, and Michael had needed a place to stay, so Michael's moving in with Rose had seemed like a mutually beneficial arrangement. I attempted to engage Michael further, but he left the apartment saying that he had another appointment to attend.

Personal Reactions

After this third session, I was forced to face several facts in regard to my approach to Rose's treatment. First, involving Rose's family in therapy was obviously going to be difficult. I had no way to contact any of her family members short of going door to door or asking Rose's neighbor Carolyn to help me find them. Yet, the family members were such an integral part of her concerns that their involvement seemed vital to the success of her treatment.

Second, my countertransference in relation to Rose's age was affecting my efforts to work with her. This interference first became apparent in the intensity of my negative reaction to Rose's sons. Whenever I thought about her case, I found myself becoming angry. Thoughts of my own grandmothers entered my mind, and I felt almost ill at the thought of them experiencing the level of hurt that Rose was currently feeling. In retrospect, I believe we were fortunate that Rose's son and grandson did not attend that second session, for I probably would have had great difficulty in joining with them in therapy. Although this type of reaction to elderly clients has been well documented (Poggi & Berland, 1985), I was nonetheless surprised by its hobbling effect on my efforts.

In addition, I found myself hesitant to confront or even reframe some of Rose's assumptions about family, gender stereotypes, and traditional gender roles. I was aware that Rose had grown up in a time that was much more conservative than today, when women's roles and men's roles were so distinct as to appear almost mutually exclusive. Furthermore, she had 79 years' worth of living that probably did little to challenge some of those assumptions. Even though her own lifestyle had varied from the traditional family model, she seemed to be labeling that lifestyle as deviant every time she apologized for it. I wondered if she knew about some of the changes in society. Did she understand what was possible now?

Did I have the legitimacy to suggest it to her? How could I, with my relative lack of experience, challenge her and her family members' truth?

Analysis

After consulting with my supervision team, I discovered that I had lost some of my therapeutic frame in my initial analysis of Rose's case. In a way, I was approaching Rose from an ageist and sexist perspective. I was ageist in assuming that Rose was out of touch and unlikely to change. I envisioned her as coming to therapy with a limited capacity to see and pursue available options. In actuality, though, Rose had given me many indications that she was interested in creating positive change in her life. She had told me during our first session that she saw therapy as a legitimate way to explore and ameliorate her unhappiness, and she had demonstrated her ability to engage in critical analysis of her own life and her role in her current life situation. I was personally challenged to realize that I had placed such arbitrary limits on my client.

I was even more challenged when I realized that my acceptance of a traditional model of family had potentially hampered my therapeutic efforts. I had perceived my inability to include Rose's relatives in therapy—to have them in the room with us—as a significant obstacle. On the one hand, I knew that changes in Rose would likely create changes in the family and that family therapy sometimes takes a more circuitous route in these types of situations. On the other hand, though, I knew that involving significant others would be an ideal way to begin addressing Rose's isolation and feelings of betrayal and abandonment.

As I worried about the details of involving family members, what I failed to see was that significant others *were* actually available to Rose. Prior to her hospitalization, Rose had been a vital member of a dynamic system—her neighborhood. As she described her connection with Carolyn, Carolyn's children, and others who lived nearby, Rose had been describing a family. Her role in this family of neighbors appeared to have been one of respected elder to whom others could come for advice and support. She had also had very practical responsibilities. Carolyn's house was essentially open all day to all people, so Rose had frequently stayed at Carolyn's to ensure that the house was secure, that neighborhood children were cared for, and that food was prepared. Carolyn's house was to the neighborhood what the kitchen is to many traditional families. Rose had chosen her place at the metaphorical heart of this family, and she had flourished.

Rose's problems had surfaced when her hospitalization triggered a series of events that challenged her place and faith in that family. Well-meaning hospital staff had ignored her string of neighborhood visitors and had instead focused on the fact that no blood kin came to visit her. As a result, Rose felt unloved and wondered if the staff thought she had been a bad mother. When her physicians asked if she had family members to help her with her recovery, Rose felt too ashamed to answer honestly. She was therefore released with the instructions to "stay home and rest," and hospital staff arranged for the occasional delivery of hot meals to Rose's apartment. Ironically, by following her physicians' advice and ensuring that she was home to receive the free meals, Rose was increasingly isolated. Then, I had entered Rose's life and started to make the same faulty assumptions and incomplete assessments as the hospital staff. I had failed to take into account the complete context of Rose's situation and had therefore dismissed her reality as well as the possibilities available to her.

Progression of Therapy

After adjusting my view of Rose, I changed my approach to our therapy. At our next session, I was honest with Rose about the imaginary limits I had placed on her and on our work together. I acknowledged my own tendency to fall back into stereotypes and tradition when confronted with new or challenging situations. Then, I asked Rose to be as involved as possible in the development of her treatment plan. I wanted to increase her sense of self-worth and agency while ensuring that my interventions and goals were relevant to her. I explained that she was the expert on her own life and that my role was to help her find solutions that made sense to her. In this way I also attempted to include both Rose's blood kin and her neighborhood family in her therapy. Finally, I asked Rose to explore her range of feelings about her blood family with the specific intention of challenging and reframing stereotyped views of herself, her family, and families in general.

Rose accepted my "confession" but seemed hesitant to take an active role in planning her treatment. She had assumed that I was an expert who could solve her problems and bring her family back together again. As we continued to talk about her desired outcomes of therapy, however, Rose increasingly showed that she had the capacity and interest to critically examine her life. I therefore encouraged her to work with me by sharing her memories of her life and family with me.

Life review is sometimes used in therapy to enhance clarity and feelings of closure for the elderly (DeGenova, 1991). In this case, as Rose reminisced I worked slowly and tentatively to help her see her life in its societal context. I encouraged her to question not necessarily herself but the stereotypes and conventions that had limited her and her family. For example, when they were young, Rose's daughters had always been responsible for housework, but her sons had not had household chores. Although Rose could recognize the inequity in that situation, this division of labor was modeled after patterns in Rose's own family of origin. As she thought about this and other such instances, Rose gradually began to wonder aloud about her children's expectations of their family roles. She was initially resistant, though, to question her own expectations of family. We eventually decided that perhaps Rose could explore that issue by talking with Carolyn and some of the neighbors about how they defined family.

Over several weeks, Rose began to increasingly involve Carolyn as an "outside" participant in our therapy sessions. In response, Carolyn helped Rose reestablish her connection with her neighborhood family. At first Rose did not want to leave her apartment for fear of leaving her grandson alone or missing a potential visit from one of her sons. Soon, though, she acknowledged that Michael was seldom home and that her sons could find her if they really wanted to do so. Carolyn arranged for several young men in the neighborhood to walk or drive Rose to Carolyn's house every day, and Rose spent less time alone in her apartment. As she began to feel less isolated, Rose's level of depression decreased. She gradually gained the capacity not only to question her feelings of disappointment with herself and her children but to claim the right to grow beyond her children's limited involvement in the family. Although Rose never rejected her children and continued to wish that the family was more connected, she began to take solace in her life with her neighbors. The idea that she and her neighbors were family gained legitimacy. As a result of her successful involvement in this new version of family, Rose's sense of failure was eased.

Rose's sons and grandson never engaged in therapy with her. When I finally had the opportunity to meet William, I was visiting Rose at Carolyn's home, and William had stopped in to see Rose. William left soon after I arrived, and I sensed that their visit had been tense and uncomfortable. Rose seemed sad after William left and indicated that she would probably always feel disappointed in how her children had "turned out." She said that she had decided, though, that families do not always love each other and often do not treat each other well. Rose seemed to be continuing to experiment with the idea that the responsibility for the family extended beyond herself and that she could likewise extend beyond her children in search of family.

Conclusion

Although this case of family therapy is perhaps somewhat unusual in its absence of traditional family work, the issues are relevant for many family practitioners working with elderly clients. The reality for many elderly people is that the idea of family must often be redefined over time. Family members die, leave, or lose their capacity to fulfill their expected roles. Frequently, the therapist's job is to attempt to understand the totality of the client's context, assess what is available to the client, and then expand the client's options. In doing so, the therapist is required to continually assess and challenge her or his own expectations regarding the elderly and to monitor the ways in which stereotypes inhibit the provision of services to this population. Feminist family therapy is especially appropriate for this age group because a feminist viewpoint encourages the therapist to question tradition and challenge oppression while working for the empowerment of the client.

References

Anderson, W. T. (1995). Four different ways to be absolutely right. In W. T. Anderson (Ed.), *The truth about the truth: De-confusing and reconstructing the post modern world* (pp. 110–116). New York: Putnam.

DeGenova, M. K. (1991). Elderly life review therapy: A Bowen approach. *American Journal of Family Therapy, 19,* 160–166.

Edinburg, M. A. (1985). *Mental health practice with the elderly.* Englewood Cliffs, NJ: Prentice Hall.

Goodrich, T. J., Rampage, C., Ellman, B., & Halstead, K. (1988). *Feminist family therapy: A casebook.* New York: Norton.

Hashimi, J. (1991). Counseling older adults. In P. K. H. Kim (Ed.), *Serving the elderly: Skills for practice* (pp. 33–50). New York: Aldine de Gruyter.

Hendricks, J., & Leedham, C. A. (1991). Theories of aging: Implications for human services. In P. K. H. Kim (Ed.), *Serving the elderly: Skills for practice* (pp. 1–25). New York: Aldine de Gruyter.

Kunkel, M. A., & Williams, C. (1991). Age and expectations about counseling: Two methodological perspectives. *Journal of Counseling and Development, 70*, 314–320.

Lorde, A. (1995). Age, race, class, and sex: Women redefining difference. In M. L. Andersen & P. H. Collins (Eds.), *Race, class, and gender* (2nd ed., pp. 532–540). Belmont, CA: Wadsworth.

McIntosh, P. (1995). White privilege and male privilege: A personal account of coming to see correspondences through work in women's studies. In M. L. Andersen & P. H. Collins (Eds.), *Race, class, and gender* (2nd ed., pp. 76–87). Belmont, CA: Wadsworth.

Monk, G. (1997). How narrative therapy works. In G. Monk, J. Winslade, K. Crocket, & D. Epston (Eds.), *Narrative therapy in practice: The archaeology of hope* (pp. 3–31). San Francisco: Jossey-Bass.

Myers, J. E. (1995). From "forgotten and ignored" to standards and certification: Gerontological counseling comes of age. *Journal of Counseling and Development, 74*, 143–149.

Poggi, R. G., & Berland, D. I. (1985). The therapists' reactions to the elderly. *The Gerontologist, 25*, 508–513.

Rathbone-McCuan, E. (1991). Family counseling: An emerging approach in clinical gerontology. In P. K. H. Kim (Ed.), *Serving the elderly: Skills for practice* (pp. 51–66). New York: Aldine de Gruyter.

Walters, M., Carter, B., Papp, P., & Silverstein, O. (1988). *The invisible web: Gender patterns in family relationships*. New York: Guilford Press.

Wimmers, M. F. H. G. (1983). Psychotherapy and counseling with the elderly: Some experiences and discussion topics. In M. Bergener (Ed.), *Geropsychiatric diagnostics and treatment* (pp. 196–205). New York: Springer.

■ ■ ■

7

Treating Couples With Anger Issues Using a Feminist Family Therapy Approach

Francesca G. Giordano, PhD
Sue Bull-Welsh, MsEd

Therapists treating couples often find themselves, directly or indirectly, helping couples work through anger with each other as part of resolving relationship difficulties. Anger can be the source of many types of conflict. Individuals may have their own difficulties with feelings of anger and reactions to such feelings. In the relationship, the couple may experience a cycle of angry feelings and reactions to each other. In this sense, anger is an integrated aspect of a pattern of dysfunctional conflict within the couple. Additionally, couples may experience angry outbursts in reaction to perceived betrayals of trust or experience the effects of suppressing angry feelings as a betrayal of trust.

This chapter examines the intersection of feminist family therapy and the treatment of anger issues in couples. Feminist family therapy offers insights into the gendered nature of anger and ways in which gender role stereotypes affect the expression of anger and the management of power within relationships. Anger and gender differences are discussed from a feminist perspective. Feminist family therapy treatment techniques and anger treatment techniques in couples counseling are reviewed. Finally, a case study is examined from a feminist family therapy perspective.

First, an understanding of aggression and violence toward women in relationships may be helpful. Of couples presenting for treatment, 50% to 70% report marital aggression in their relationships, and almost 25% have experienced acts of physical aggression during the marriage (Vivian & Langhinrichsen-Rohling, 1994). As a result, the professional literature and program development regarding anger have focused on conceptualizing or treating domestic violence (Pagelow, 1984). The link between domestic violence treatment and anger management is clear. Often batterers are unable to manage their angry feelings, and resulting conflicts escalate into violence. The domestic violence literature highlights anger and aggression management (Cullen & Freeman-Longo, 1996). However, there are two limitations in this literature. First, it does not examine anger from a feminist perspective. Second, it does not specifically target couples who may be at risk for physical abuse but currently are only experiencing conflict and relational pain. This chapter specifically addresses both these issues but does not explore domestic violence per se. The ideas explored in this chapter are not meant to suggest that women should stay in unhealthy and dangerous relationships.

The Nature of Anger

Anger is an emotion that varies greatly in intensity, ranging from annoyance to rage. Current theories suggest three aspects of emotional response: Emotions have unique characteristics; they are used as information on how an internal or external event is experienced; and they play a role in interactions with others. Malatesta and Izard (1984) suggested that, like other emotions, anger has three basic characteristics: physiological, behavioral, and subjective characteristics. The exact manifestation of these characteristics varies tremendously from individual to individual. Both men and women can increase their awareness of how and when they are angry by examining subtle aspects of changes in thought and behavior.

A cognitive–behavioral perspective that does not adequately account for the role of gender has dominated the theoretical understanding of the nature of anger. This perspective suggests that men and women experience angry feelings within a similar cognitive context and that these cognitions lead individuals to conclusions about the impact of internal or external events. In short, individuals "decide" to be angry on the basis of their cognitive appraisal. Nowhere in this perspective of anger, however, is the concept of cognitive appraisal in a gendered context.

Although the cognitive–behavioral perspective on anger has dominated the research and treatment literature, there are two other important theoretical orientations with different perspectives. Humanistic views of anger emphasize its "orienting" properties, in which the impact of an individual or an event is conveyed through emotions (Greenberg & Safran, 1989; Rogers, 1961). This perspective emphasizes the information aspect of anger, in that the information conveyed by angry feelings suggests an emotional reaction. An interactional orientation focuses on anger as a response to transactions among persons with an emphasis on interpersonal interactions (Averill, 1982; DeRivera, 1984). Anger helps people interpret relationships and may serve as a catalyst to change such relationships. This perspective of anger has dominated the treatment literature on conflicts in couples. The cyclic nature of this interpretation of anger lends itself to a systemic analysis that emphasizes patterns (including communication patterns) within relationships.

These differing perspectives on the nature of anger and its treatment are strangely united on the context in which anger is felt. People who perceive that their rights or boundaries have been violated feel anger in the context of power and control. Anger is associated with interpersonal situations in which a person feels wronged or unjustly treated, although these conclusions may be based on distorted cognitions. Anger is felt when an undesired or undeserved outcome is experienced. Anger can indicate potential violence, hostility, and aggression. In couples, anger is directly linked to relational injury, betrayal, and violations of trust. As a result, when treating couples with anger issues, the therapist is always working within the context of power and control. Feminist family therapy, with its application of feminist theory to the treatment of couples and special emphasis on the social context as a prime determinant of behavior, is uniquely positioned to understand the context of power and control within a couple and its manifestation on couple interactions.

The understanding of anger from a feminist perspective includes aspects of cognitive–behavioral, humanistic, and interactional theories. Miller (1991), in her foundational exploration of the feminist construction of anger, viewed it as an aspect of the gendered nature of the self. As with all emotions, anger is felt by both men and women, but the effects of gender role stereotypes, women's development, and the implications of anger in issues of power and control have a tremendous effect on the experience and expression of anger. Miller suggested that women are taught to minimize and suppress their angry feelings, whereas men are taught to exaggerate and express theirs as a method of legitimizing and maintaining a male-centered society. This maintenance of cultural equilibrium manifests itself in the beliefs men and women have about their anger, the style in which they express anger, the reaction of others to their anger, and behavioral reactions to their own angry feelings. Feminist family therapy suggests that these dynamics manifest themselves within couples' conflicts and that gender role socialization teaches women to limit their understanding of the implications of their anger.

Dynamics of Anger in Women

Theorists in the psychology of women have suggested that relationship orientation is a foundational aspect of women's development. Many researchers have suggested that attachment and care are equal in importance to autonomy and independence in the lives of well-adjusted women (Chodorow, 1978; McClelland, 1975; Miller, 1976). Anger normally results when relationships are troubled, but a strong relationship orientation may lead some women to suppress anger rather than risk challenging relationships, especially when these relationships are intertwined with their sense of self (Bernardez-Bonesatti, 1978). Horner (1979) suggested that conflicts in relationships are difficult for women because the risk of separation evokes feelings of disorganization and dissolution of self. As a result, women deny or minimize their angry feelings to protect their sense of self. Additionally, women's feelings of responsibility and care for others often lead them to inappropriately enmeshed boundaries and an exaggerated sense of responsibility for others (Lerner, 1985; Miller, 1991; Thomas, 1993). They may deny they are angry to protect others or to take responsibility for change away from others.

Negative social messages about the acceptability of expressing anger are another issue especially affecting women. Miller (1991) and Lerner (1985) suggested that women, as an oppressed group, have been taught that they have no cause to be angry and that if they feel anger, the fault must be with them. As a result, women develop belief systems denying their right to their own anger. When a woman feels anger, her belief system inhibits action. Women often feel that anger is only appropriate when felt in someone else's defense (Miller, 1991). These social messages can cause women to deny angry feelings in themselves or keep them from positive self-directed change. Suppressed anger may thus be linked to clinical manifestations focused on the denial of self, such as depression, low self-esteem, and eating disorders (Thomas, 1993).

Finally, the literature indicates a link between feelings of anger and women's experiences with injustice and oppression (Miller, 1991). For example, as part of recovery from physical and sexual abuse, women often feel intense anger toward the perpetrator. This anger results from a felt injustice. Similarly, women's experiences with sexism may evoke angry feelings, but this link is most often associated with racism and multicultural issues (Grier & Cobbs, 1968; Watson, 1989), especially in the development of racial identity (Cross, 1991; Helms, 1990). Travis (1989) suggested that anger is associated with experiences of betrayal, especially in relationships. Anger in women may be a natural response to a social position of decreased personal power; when anger over injustice is turned to denial and self-blame, psychological distress will often result.

Dynamics of Anger in Men

Anger in men also is seen as a core self issue, rooted in the gendered nature of the self. Definitions of maleness include separateness from others, rationality, competence, control, power over others, and competitiveness (Dienhart & Myers-Avis, 1991). These characteristics directly inform men's difficulties with the healthy expression of anger and its link to aggressive behaviors. Miller (1991) suggested that in men's psychological development, young boys are taught not to express feelings as emotions. Instead, boys are encouraged to act out emotions in physical play and aggressiveness. However, anger may have a unique dynamic in this developmental process. Young boys may be taught that the feeling and expression of anger are acceptable (in contrast to other emotions such as fear or sadness), and the expression of anger through aggressive behavior is encouraged. When masculinity is constructed as mastery of the environment and others through competitiveness, boys are made to fear not being aggressive. As a result, feelings that evoke aggressive responses are reinforced and rewarded.

Chodorow (1978) characterized the core of male socialization as a process of separating from the primary caregiver. Men carry this internalized sense of separateness throughout their lives. From this perspective, it is clear that for men anger becomes the emotion of choice.

Furthermore, anger creates separation in relationships (Bernardez-Bonesatti, 1978; Horner, 1979). Anger is common in troubled relationships, especially around issues of trust and boundaries. Men may feel comforted by anger, because anger reinforces that the self can be maintained in the absence of intimacy. Anger creates more "psychological breathing room" in which the self can be experienced as whole and complete. As a result, there may be evidence that men feel anger as a defensive response to perceived threats to their masculinity. When men feel defeated by others, when there is a perceived loss in a competition or a loss of control over a situation, or if women ask for vulnerability in relationships, men may experience these situations as damage to the core self and as threats to their masculinity. Getting angry and acting out that anger may help to restore a sense of mastery of self, others, and environment. Additionally, anger may often be felt in conjunction with hurt, humiliation, vulnerability, impotence, embarrassment, and isolation—all feelings that can be seen as threats to a masculine self. Thus, anger is viewed as a safe emotional response, one that blocks other more threatening emotions.

Similarly, Ganley (1991) suggested that men are oversocialized in using anger as a mask for other emotions. Travis (1989) also connected these themes in men's anger, commenting that men's anger is instrumental rather than relational. Men use anger to control, to intimidate, to punish—in general, to accomplish a task. Even in sports, as in other types of competitive activities, men's anger is used as a motivator to win. This can be linked to men's socialization to be competitive and dominant. Gender role socialization of men actively creates and reinforces men's dominant position over women, also reinforcing aggressive responses to anger as normal (Goodrich, Rampage, Ellman, & Halstead, 1988).

Finally, there is indication of a link between feelings of anger and men's socialization to entitlement (Ganley, 1991). Anger often is felt in relation to perceptions of being wronged, being treated unjustly, or not being given what one deserves. If men are socialized to view interactions with women as something to which they are entitled, they will feel anger when denied or at any occurrence in a relationship that negates their sense of control. Anger and aggression may therefore be linked to distorted beliefs regarding entitlement and control of others.

Treatment Strategies for Couples

Differences in men's and women's psychological development and socialization have had a profound effect on the role of anger in their lives. Gender constructs anger-generated behaviors in women and men. Themes of anger, boundary violation, injustice, unmet needs, and other perceived wrongs are often the themes of relational injury in couples. Treatment strategies that target anger from a feminist family therapy perspective are useful when couples have experienced cycles of angry outbursts and aggressive reactions, when violation of trust and other types of relational injury have occurred, or when one or both members of the couple have difficulties with anger. There is a systemic assumption embedded in this conceptualization, suggesting that when one member of a couple experiences "problems with anger," both members need treatment.

Using Emotional Expression to Equalize Power

Both men and women have difficulties recognizing and expressing anger, although sex role socialization would suggest that their difficulties represent opposite ends of the same continuum. Women underreact to angry feelings; they have a propensity to express anger through somatic symptoms, such as headaches (Thomas, 1993). Although women may be better than men at recognizing other types of feelings in themselves (such as sadness and fear), they are less likely to recognize anger. Women also are often more attuned to the feelings of others, especially a partner. Men, on the other hand, are more likely to overreact to their angry feelings, expressing anger instead of other emotions. They also are less likely to recognize any feelings in themselves and others. Women and men often have opposite styles in the expression of anger. Women "stuff" their anger, whereas men "escalate" their anger (Weisinger, 1985). Feminist family therapy suggests that these characteristics alone create power imbalances that damage relationships.

Often these power imbalances create a spiraling cycle, in which women's lack of awareness of angry feelings leads to suppressed anger, producing frustration and inaction that lead to increased feelings of weakness and low self-esteem. Women may become more and more filled with unacknowledged anger, leading eventually to the expression of anger in exaggerated forms, such as screaming and yelling (Miller, 1991). Men have their own spiraling cycle, in which overreaction to angry feelings or expression of anger instead of other feelings leads to verbally or physically aggressive behaviors. Men become more and more filled with unacknowledged fear or sadness, producing increased feelings of insecurity that lead to increases in controlling behaviors (Cullen & Freeman-Longo, 1996).

Both members of the couple must be taught feeling recognition. Activities designed to evoke angry feelings, to explore the effects of suppressed anger, and to develop skills in recognizing anger may help women who report feeling constant anger as well as women who report never feeling angry. For men, activities designed to evoke feelings other than anger, to develop skills to recognize a range of feelings, and to explore the effects of escalated anger are recommended. Teaching couples to work together also can be useful. Couples can keep daily journals of nonverbal expression of feelings and discuss the entries with each other. The sharing of dreams, music, drawings, books, and movies as external experiences to evoke discussion around differences in emotional expression and reaction to angry feelings is also important. The key is encouraging the couple to work together on feeling recognition and expression assignments, each with their own strengths. Men help women recognize anger; women help men recognize other feelings. These exercises also tend to increase the empowerment of women by using and emphasizing feeling recognition skills. At this time, it is important to discourage women from moving on to "taking care of feelings." Keeping the exercises focused away from "action" also encourages men to reflect on their anger, rather than quickly jumping from anger to control.

Confronting Gender Role Stereotyped Belief Systems

Beck (1976) suggested that cognitive appraisal plays a powerful role in determining a person's emotional response to any situation. Therefore, women's and men's beliefs about the validity of their anger may mediate its expression. Many different types of beliefs prevent, interfere with, or distort the direct awareness and expression of anger. Many of these belief systems stem from the messages society gives men and women. Miller (1991) suggested that when women have negative beliefs about themselves, their beliefs deflect their anger away from the actual source and onto the women themselves. In this way, these beliefs distort feelings of anger into a personal sense of defectiveness, irrationality, and worthlessness (Miller, 1991). Women also may have adopted belief systems from family, religious training, and society, reinforcing the concept of anger in themselves as inappropriate, sinful, or wrong.

Men also have belief systems that distort their anger feelings. Some men get angry or act out their anger in aggressive behaviors because they have adopted a belief system that these reactions make them more masculine. Others believe that masculinity is rooted in "rationality" and suppress anger into logical responses or a belief that a man's role is to protect women from potential harm, and, therefore, suppressing anger reduces the risk of hurtful or aggressive behaviors.

The family is the major source of socialization of gender role behaviors (Goodrich et al., 1988). As a result, the therapist can facilitate an exploration of belief systems by asking each member of the couple to explore (with each other) how their mothers and fathers expressed anger. Often this analysis reveals the stereotypical gender role belief systems that maintain the couple's difficulties. A genogram may help to explore family patterns of expression of anger and their consequences. Social analysis is another useful tool in this process (Russell, 1984). During social analysis, each member of the couple is asked to list all of the messages she or he has received, positive and negative, about anger and its expression from social and cultural influences. Then, they explore the consequences of these messages. Russell suggested that this process could help clients link feelings of helplessness or powerlessness to social conditioning rather than to personal inadequacy. In this process, belief systems that support psychological health can be reinforced, whereas more restrictive belief systems can be confronted and reframed.

Focusing on Relationship Versus Achievement Needs

The integration and balance of relationship and achievement needs is a major developmental task for adults, and no other issue more powerfully reflects the impact of the disparate sex role socialization of men and women (Ganley, 1991). Women are socialized to value relationships and see their own need fulfillment in this light. Men construct their needs more clearly in terms of task achievement, often to the extent of damaging their relationships. This dynamic sets up a common pattern in the relationships of men and women. Women overfunction around relationship tasks and underfunction around achievement tasks, whereas men suffer from the reverse. As a result, women feel responsible for the nature of the relationship and may neglect their own achievement needs to refocus on the needs of their partner; paradoxically, in this effort to reduce anxiety about their own achievement needs, women may thus neglect them further. Women may have been socialized into accepting the following two messages that support men's achievement needs and women's relationship needs: "Your own needs are best fulfilled when the achievement needs of your spouse are fulfilled" and "Your own needs are best fulfilled when your relationships are intimate and happy." Traditional gender role construction suggests that, even when women work outside the home, their own career and personal needs are treated as second in importance to those of their spouses (Goodrich et al., 1988).

Anger is a signal that something must be changed (Lerner, 1985). Anger is the emotional messenger that tells clients something is wrong, that something hurts, or that one is experiencing a violation. Giordano (1997) suggested that anger is a powerful message that one's needs are not being met. In this sense, angry feelings can be reframed from feelings that alienate others and cause conflicts to signals for necessary, positive, action-oriented goals. These unmet needs often focus on "high-level" issues of self-esteem, such as respect, significance, honor, expertise, love, and a sense of belonging. For example, feelings about abandonment during early childhood may be expressed during adult years as anger about unmet needs for security and love. Many women may find themselves continually angry because they feel they are not valued, respected, or loved for their special qualities, significance, or knowledge. Their anger is a message that these needs remain unmet.

Examination of the "message" in women's anger about unmet needs and the suggestion that these messages have action-taking potential can be an excellent therapeutic tool to overcome the effects of sex role socialization of both women and men. Therapists can pinpoint the exact nature of the unmet needs signaled by anger by asking open-ended questions about how needs are filled in the life of the couple. Careful probing should focus on both relationship needs and achievement needs. For example, asking both women and men about feeling loved, respected, and valued might bring out the need for more love, respect, or value in their lives. Listening carefully to stories about anger-provoking episodes will prove helpful in offering insights about unmet needs, wants, or desires. The therapist can suggest a more equal balance of tasks to meet achievement and relationship needs for both members. Therapists can help their clients "decode" their angry messages into information about new behaviors or activities to be implemented.

Problem-solving techniques for angry feelings represent a shift from a need for change to actual changes. Problem-solving techniques acknowledge angry feelings as motivators for change. Once motivators have been pinpointed, goals for change can be identified and implemented. Therapists can assign specific actions as "homework assignments" and explore the results during subsequent sessions. This type of problem-solving technique can help couples move toward action by developing short-term goals. Anger messages often signal the absence of an important force, such as respect, healthy treatment, or fair performance expectations, especially for women. Worell and Remer (1992) suggested that helping women set healthy and positive self-care goals for themselves is a first step toward empowering them. This constructive use of anger may also help develop new interaction patterns to break up the cycles of overfunctioning and underfunctioning in the relationship.

Using Anger to Protect Boundaries

People often feel angry when their rights and boundaries have been violated. Especially for women, anger can be a signal of the "deselfing" phenomenon in their lives (Jack, 1991; Lerner, 1985), in which women sacrifice their own desires to preserve harmony with others. Men experience anger about boundary violation as well. A boundary violation can be defined as any experience in which self-definition is ignored or violated. It is clear that physical violation, such as physical or sexual violence, is a violation of self, although any experience in which a person requires too much or expects too little from another can be seen as a type of boundary violation.

As Lerner (1985) and others have suggested, sometimes cycles of anger and conflicts in couples are reactions to violations and other experiences with powerlessness from childhood. From the perspective of contextual family therapy, children who have been victims of family violence often harbor extensive feelings of distrust of others (Boszormenyi-Nagy & Krasner, 1986). These victims, for whom love and trust have been violated in the past, transform such feelings into negative impressions of themselves and their relationships in the here and now (Hargrave, 1994). For both men and women, anger is a residual effect of these damaging experiences, used to keep others at a distance. In a sense, the angry feelings and subsequent aggressive behaviors (especially for men) are a way of saying "Don't come near me, I've been hurt before."

In women, angry feelings about boundary violations can also be linked to role overload. Lerner (1985) connected these concepts to responsibility, suggesting that women may overfunction or underfunction in relationships, taking too little or too much responsibility for the actions of others. The effects of trying to be super moms, super workers, and super mates can lead to overwhelming performance expectations (Giordano, 1995). Thomas (1993) suggested that perceived stress—the degree to which a woman feels overloaded and out of control—is important in the cognitive appraisal linked to feelings of anger. In the same way, experiences in which women's qualities and characteristics are underestimated or made to appear childlike are boundary violations.

Men experience feelings of anger triggered by role conflicts as well. Men are more likely to experience role conflict than role overload. In this sense, men may feel anger when expectations of their roles as fathers, lovers, and providers seem to be changing. This perceived absence of control or powerlessness evokes strong feelings of anger. There is some evidence that this type of gender role strain is on the increase for men (Brooks, 1991).

In couples, cycles of angry feelings can represent either current experiences of role overload and gender role strain or past experiences with boundary violations, manifesting themselves in an absence of trust. Therapists can work with couples to help them identify the connection between past and present boundary violations and anger. To identify the exact nature of the boundary violation, therapists can generate lists of task responsibility, ask open-ended questions about what the couple want for themselves versus what they want for each other, and use insight-oriented responses. In feminist family therapy, it is especially important to increase men's empathy toward the variety of boundary-violating experiences that occur for women. Often men's ability to easily access their anger regarding their own boundary violations can help facilitate such empathy. Additionally, an analysis of role responsibility can help equalize role expectations and family burdens for both men and women.

Working on Issues of Injustice and the Role of Destructive Entitlement

Much of the literature on anger has linked feelings of anger to experiences with injustice (Giordano, 1997; Travis, 1989). When anger over perceived injustice manifests itself in couples' conflicts, it is often a complex interaction of many different factors. Women's anger is often rooted in actual injustice—unequal treatment based on gender. Men's anger often can be rooted in perceived injustice that stems from a distorted sense of entitlement, wherein men believe that they have "rights" to women and control over women's behavior. This destructive entitlement can manifest itself in paranoid attitudes, hostility, and rage and is rooted in the idea that people have an innate sense of justice (Boszormenyi-Nagy & Krasner, 1986). This innate sense of justice demands balance between what people are entitled to receive from a relationship and what they are obliged to give. Damaged family-of-origin relationships can lead to skewed views of what constitutes a "just" relationship, creating a situation in which an innate sense of justice manifests itself distortedly, as a need for revenge or control.

These issues around justice for men and women intersect with anger. People have a belief in a just and fair world. Travis (1989) argued that clients will use beliefs that "the world is fair" and that "people get what they deserve" to organize experience, to make sense out of confusion, to synthesize justice out of cruelty and unfairness, and to create orderliness out of random events. To maintain a just-world belief system, women use cognitive distortions to block anger, whereas men use cognitive distortions to escalate anger. Examples of such distortions include blaming or denigrating victims, reinterpreting events and outcomes so that justice seems served or moral growth encouraged, and using denial to block out unpleasant information.

Abusive men's anger may be integrated into an internalized belief that aggressiveness is justified because it forces relationships to match a distorted standard of justice and fairness (Jory, Anderson, & Greer, 1997). Feminist family therapists can challenge and confront men on the construction of a just relationship, integrating three dimensions of justice: equality, fairness, and caring. An actual just and fair relationship would thus include such qualities as mutual freedom, reciprocity, empathy, respect, accountability, mutuality, accommodation, attachment, and nurturance. Particularly important aspects of relationships to be challenged are gender domination and the way in which stereotypes of masculinity and femininity undermine personal responsibility for abuse and violence (Jenkins, 1990). Therapists must encourage women to give voice to the effects abusive relationships have on them, as women can sometimes share or are compliant with such distorted perspectives on justice and fairness. Gender socialization that encourages women to blame themselves for any difficulties in relationships and a just-world belief system that silences their anger often leave women with difficulty in expressing their feelings of anger, fear, and sadness. Using feminist family therapy principles, therapists are encouraged to oppose the distorted concept of "just" relationships, which perpetuates disempowerment and abuse of women. Encouraging men to develop increased empathy for the feelings of women facilitates understanding of the role of mutuality, nurturance, and accommodation in relationships. However, these confrontations must be conducted within trusting and respectful healing relationships. Therapists must always maintain the credibility to offer alternatives, to help remove destructive entitlement belief systems, and to encourage novel, unfamiliar solutions (Goodrich et al., 1988).

In working with women's anger stemming from unjust relationships, the therapist's first step is to help the client acknowledge the actuality of injustice. Then, positive change can be implemented by encouraging adaptive responses to the experience. Choosing adaptive rather than nonadaptive responses to an unjust experience often alleviates the anger. Just as men may maintain relationships through destructive entitlement belief systems, women may perpetuate the same abusive, neglecting dynamics through an inability to recognize their own worthiness for equality, fairness, and caring. Such beliefs can lead to increased oppositional responses, in which women are resistant to change, experience angry outbursts or increased passivity, and sometimes exhibit violent or self-injurious behavior. When working with women experiencing anger about injustice, therapists may find that an action-taking, problem-solving approach can be valuable. Injustices often are experienced on a deeply personal level, leaving women feeling extremely vulnerable and out of control. Encouraging positive actions can help mediate against these negative responses and increase women's sense of safety and control.

Developing Gender-Fair Communication Skills

Finally, therapists are cautioned against viewing anger difficulties in couples as simply the result of a lack of adequate conflict resolution and communication skills. Couples often need communication skills training, but overemphasis on direct expression of angry feelings may mask power dynamics in relationships and encourage women to express their anger using male-normed communication techniques (Miller, 1976), which merely reverses the problem while doing little to correct it. This can be avoided by using communication models that focus on process-oriented communication strategies, which are more sensitive to a gendered perspective. Couples can be encouraged to shift from content communicating to process communicating. A content-to-process shift asks the communicator to stop discussing the *what* of a message and focus on *how* the communication process is happening. In this sense, power dynamics may be revealed and can be brought up for discussion.

A Couple With Anger Issues

The case of Jan and Todd suggests several themes common to couples with angry outbursts as part of their marital conflict. On review, aspects of their case history illustrate several themes common to such couples. Jan is a 22-year-old, married, Caucasian woman who was 2 months pregnant at the time of intake. She was referred to the community mental health agency from a local hospital after her husband called the police and had her taken to the emergency room for a suicidal verbal threat.

Jan's presenting concerns focused on marital problems with her husband. She stated that ever since she told her husband she was pregnant, he had been yelling at her. She reported that there was no physical abuse, but she did say that he had pushed her down on the couch over 2 months ago and had blocked her way out of rooms on occasion, when he wasn't finished "saying what he has to." He had not attended any prenatal visits and threatened to leave her 2 days ago. She reported that she was so upset that she told him she was going to kill herself. During the assessment, she admitted that she never intended to do so but was only trying to keep him from leaving her. She stated she felt lonely and sad because her husband was gone without explanation for 2 days. She complained of vomiting and crying for those 2 days. She reported that she felt alone with the pregnancy, which made her feel angry. She described her home life as "cold, distant, lonely, loud, and angry" and said that she "felt more like a roommate than a wife."

Jan was born in Kentucky, and when she was 2 years of age, her biological parents divorced. She has one biological sister, one half sister, and one stepbrother. Both parents remarried, with her father living in Kentucky and her mother currently living 1 hour away. Jan is married to Todd (age 28), who has a bachelor's degree and owns and teaches in a karate school. He has three sons from a previous marriage (4, 6, and 9 years old). Todd and Jan have been married 1 year. Jan has her associate's degree in computer science and works part-time at a local YMCA.

Jan attended several counseling sessions alone and several with Todd. During the first session, after Todd's return home, Jan appeared happier and more relaxed. She stated that he had not spoken about their verbal fighting. She said she wanted to be able to tell him how she was feeling and not ignore their problems. She talked of becoming so upset when she was angry that she could not speak. Sometimes she resorted to name calling. She identified with her mother and father-in-law, both of whom use the same expression style when angry.

After canceling her next two scheduled appointments, Jan arrived for her second session and stated Todd had been spending increasing amounts of time with her and paying more attention to her. She reported that he had been speaking more about their upcoming baby. The therapist encouraged Jan not to ignore her and Todd's struggles with angry outbursts and recommended that he join her for couples counseling. Jan was given a homework assignment to work on an anger journal and to share the assignment with Todd by asking him to work on his own journal.

During her third session, Jan reported she had not worked on her journal and had not discussed couples counseling with Todd. She stated that she was angry with Todd's ex-wife. She had tried to talk to Todd about her feelings but stated that it was late when she tried to talk with him. During the conversation, he was reading, and she was "asking him questions." Jan stated she was feeling concerned about her three stepsons because of their anger and violence toward one another. She told the therapist that the two older boys had been diagnosed with attention deficit hyperactivity disorder and were taking Ritalin. Jan spoke of not getting along with the boys because they were "too close" with their biological mother.

After canceling another appointment, Jan and Todd arrived for couples counseling. They talked about stress as the source of their anger—mostly financial issues and Todd's three sons. They stated that they did not have enough money to pay bills because Todd was not being fairly compensated at work. Todd said he was a "workaholic" like his father and his brothers. They both spoke of discipline concerns with the boys. Todd admitted being more lenient on the boys than Jan was. Todd said he instilled in the boys a value of the importance of family. Todd, who is a black belt in karate, gave each son a set of boxing gloves as a gift last Christmas. Jan and Todd said they let the two older boys wrestle supervised on a mat at the karate school. Both seemed reluctant to discuss their relationship with each other.

Jan and Todd attended the next session together but stated that Todd would no longer attend sessions because of his heavy work schedule. They reported getting ready to move to a new town closer to the karate school and Jan's mother, who could help with the new baby. Both were excited about the move and stated that they had an equal part in the decision-making process. Jan reported that she and Todd were getting along better lately, taking some time to relax together and talk more openly about what they want. Todd stated that because of work, he probably would not be of much help with the new baby. Jan said that Todd sometimes teases her about her nervousness with childbirth, but he stops when she tells him to. Todd agreed to take a week off work when the baby was born. Jan told him she wanted him to be involved in the birth of the baby and voiced concern that he would "really not work" for a whole week.

They both discussed Jan's anger at her stepfather because he refused to help them with a loan, reportedly saying: "When your marriage fails, I won't be stuck with your debt." They agreed that Jan was much more enraged by this statement than Todd was. She stated that he hurt her feelings and she would not speak to him until he apologized. She indicated that she tries to get along with her stepfather for her mother's sake. Jan said that her mother feels that it is the woman's responsibility to keep the home nice for her man. Jan commented, "I don't want that. I know what I want and what my husband wants, so it doesn't matter what anyone else thinks." She stated that she does not expect to speak to her stepfather because she "doesn't care." She commented that "he knows I'm hurt, and it's not worth my time to argue. He knows I'm upset and that's good enough for me." She stated that she told her mother how she was feeling and her mother relayed that to her husband.

During Jan's final session, she said that her relationship with Todd was "going fine" but that she still felt she was doing everything herself. She commented, "I'm by myself. I never see him, and that can never be changed." She felt that she had continued to yell and cry on occasion, but she does not wish to start an argument where nothing gets resolved. She denied the suggestion that she is avoiding her own anger and conflicts with Todd and her stepfather.

Case Analysis Using Feminist Family Therapy Principles

During supervision sessions between the authors of this chapter, the following themes were discussed:

1. Jan and Todd's anger toward each other, especially around the birth of their child, illustrates the common need-based dynamic of achievement versus relationship. Jan is angry about Todd's lack of involvement with the baby's birth, which Todd sees as "justified" because the couple's financial concerns "force" him to work long hours. Todd is angry at Jan for not understanding that his work is for the "good of both of them." Todd gets his achievement needs met, whereas Jan's relationship needs seem unmet, unless Todd participates in the "birth of the baby." Jan's achievement needs remain unspoken, perhaps indirectly suggested by her anger at her stepfather. An exploration of their anger as a signal of unmet needs could reveal this dynamic.

2. Jan and Todd manifest anger around role conflict. It is difficult for them to discuss this conflict directly, but they can indirectly touch on it when discussing conflicts around raising Todd's sons. Jan's role overload results from her being the one completely responsible for household upkeep, raising three stepsons, preparing for the birth of their baby, and working part-time. Todd seems somewhat confused and conflicted about his role as a father. This may be manifested in the indirect expression of anger and aggression around child-rearing issues. He nurtures his sons with karate lessons and "teases" Jan about childbirth.

3. Both Jan and Todd use gender role stereotypical ways of expressing their anger. Todd's anger shows itself in aggressive acts and "working too hard." Jan avoids direct conflict with her stepfather while using ineffective anger expression techniques with Todd. When her anger seems to threaten her relationships, she increases her ability to "take it on" and seemingly becomes more compromising in decision making.

4. The case offers a clear example of how styles of anger expression can be intergenerationally transmitted. Jan and Todd seem to manifest the same stereotypical gender role anger expression style as their parents. Jan mimics the style of her mother, whereas Todd uses his father's approach of acting out anger. Both seem to be transmitting this style to their children. Lifestyle conflicts between parent and adult-child generations can be used as beginning points for discussion about problems associated with stereotypical anger expression styles. Mother and father enact traditional gender roles and teach their sons to do so as well. Todd and Jan have expressed the desire "not to be like their parents." This thought can be used to open a discussion about the similar patterns in anger expression, but the therapist must be careful and use a nonthreatening approach.

5. Todd manifests some characteristics associated with men feeling anger around entitlement issues. His anger and threats to leave Jan often occur when she complains about his behavior. Todd believes that he has a right to determine how much he participates in his family life and that Jan's "difficulty" is her failure to accede to his choices. This sense of entitlement can often escalate into domestic violence. As a couple, they illustrate a common dilemma: Jan presents with an "anger problem," but the more serious anger issues really lie with Todd. Todd may be beginning to manifest disempowering behaviors

toward Jan, representing an unjust, controlling belief system regarding how one should treat one's (female) partner. Todd could be confronted about ways in which his sense of entitlement represents an absence of empathy toward Jan. Todd could be asked to rethink what respecting Jan might mean about his behavior. Todd's belief in "family values" could be a cognitive set on which to begin this work.

6. Jan and Todd's anger toward each other seemed resolved when the decision was made to move closer to Jan's mother and Todd's work site. At this point, they also began spending more time together "working on the relationship." This construction of their relationship can be seen to reinforce traditional cultural expectations of women as primary caretakers and men as primary providers. It also depicts men as central to decision making and power, whereas women are central to family life and accommodators to decisions. Jan's final session serves as evidence that this resolution of their conflicts will deflect rather than resolve Jan's anger and that it will likely reappear in future conflicts.

Conclusion

Therapists who wish to help couples work through cycles of anger and conflict must be familiar with the unique characteristics of anger as an emotion and the sociopsychological dynamics of anger in the lives of women and men. Feminist family therapy offers insightful analysis and powerful techniques that enable therapists to expose the underlying gender dynamics embedded in angry feelings and passive or aggressive reactions. Often techniques based on simple cognitive–behavioral constructs of anger do not rid clients of their angry feelings toward each other and misdirect the source of these feelings to the individual and away from implications of society's construct of gender and its influence on the development of the self. The techniques suggested in this chapter may aid therapists by adding to the depth of their understanding of the anger dynamic in couples and their ability to support clients' change to less angry and conflicted relational interactions.

References

Averill, J. R. (1982). *Anger and aggression: An essay on emotion.* New York: Springer-Verlag.

Beck, A. (1976). *Cognitive therapy and the emotional disorders.* New York: International Universities Press.

Bernardez-Bonesatti, T. (1978). Women and anger: Conflicts with aggression in contemporary women. *Journal of the American Medical Women's Association, 33,* 215–219.

Boszormenyi-Nagy, I., & Krasner, B. (1986). *Between give and take: A clinical guide to contextual therapy.* New York: Brunner/Mazel.

Brooks, G. R. (1991). Traditional men in marital and family therapy. In M. Bograd (Ed.), *Feminist approaches for men in family therapy* (pp. 51–73). New York: Haworth Press.

Chodorow, N. (1978). *The reproduction of mothering.* Berkeley: University of California Press.

Cross, W. (1991). *Shades of black.* Philadelphia: Temple University Press.

Cullen, M., & Freeman-Longo, R. E. (1996). *Men and anger: Understanding and managing your anger for a much better life.* Brandon, VT: Safer Society Press.

DeRivera, J. (1984). Development and the full range of emotional experience. In C. A. Malatesta & C. E. Izard (Eds.), *Emotion in adult development* (pp. 45–63). Beverly Hills, CA: Sage.

Dienhart, A., & Myers-Avis, J. (1991). Men in therapy: Exploring feminist-informed alternatives. In M. Bograd (Ed.), *Feminist approaches for men in family therapy* (pp. 25–49). New York: Haworth Press.

Ganley, A. (1991). Feminist therapy with male clients. In M. Bograd (Ed.), *Feminist approaches for men in family therapy* (pp. 1–23). New York: Haworth Press.

Giordano, F. G. (1995). The whole person at work: An integrative vocational intervention model for women's workplace issues. *Journal for Specialists in Group Work, 20,* 4–13.

Giordano, F. G. (1997). Therapeutic interventions for managing anger in women. *Directions in Clinical and Counseling Psychology, 7*(14), 3–15.

Goodrich, T. J., Rampage, C., Ellman, B., & Halstead, K. (1988). *Feminist family therapy: A casebook.* New York: Norton.

Greenberg, L., & Safran, J. (1989). Emotion in psychotherapy. *American Psychologist, 44,* 19–29.

Grier, W., & Cobbs, P. (1968). *Black rage.* New York: Basic Books.

Hargrave, T. (1994). Families and forgiveness: A theoretical and therapeutic framework. *Family Journal, 2,* 339–348.

Helms, J. (1990). *Black and White racial identity.* Westport, CT: Greenwood.

Horner, A. J. (1979). *Object relations and the developing ego in therapy.* New York: Jason Aronson.

Jack, D. C. (1991). *Silencing the self.* Cambridge, MA: Harvard University Press.

Jenkins, A. (1990). *Invitations to responsibility: The therapeutic engagement of men who are violent and abusive.* Adelaide, South Australia: Dulwich Centre.

Jory, B., Anderson, D., & Greer, C. (1997). Intimate justice: Confronting issues of accountability, respect, and freedom in treatment for abuse and violence. *Journal of Marital and Family Therapy, 23*, 399–419.

Lerner, H. G. (1985). *The dance of anger: A woman's guide to changing the patterns of intimate relationships.* New York: Harper & Row.

Malatesta, C. A., & Izard, C. E. (1984). Introduction: Conceptualizing emotional development in adults. In C. A. Malatesta & C. E. Izard (Eds.), *Emotion in adult development* (pp. 13–21). Beverly Hills, CA: Sage.

McClelland, D. (1975). *Power: The inner experience.* New York: Irvington.

Miller, J. B. (1976). *Toward a new psychology of women.* Boston: Beacon Press.

Miller, J. B. (1991). The construction of anger in women and men. In J. Jordan, A. Kaplan, J. B. Miller, I. Striver, & J. Surrey (Eds.), *Women's growth in connection: Writings from the Stone Center* (pp. 181–196). New York: Guilford Press.

Pagelow, M. D. (1984). *Family violence.* New York: Praeger.

Rogers, C. R. (1961). *On becoming a person.* Boston: Houghton Mifflin.

Russell, M. N. (1984). *Skills in counseling women: The feminist approach.* Springfield, IL: Charles C Thomas.

Thomas, S. P. (1993). *Women and anger.* New York: Springer.

Travis, C. (1989). *Anger: The misunderstood emotion.* New York: Simon & Schuster.

Vivian, D., & Langhinrichsen-Rohling, J. (1994). Are bi-directionally violent couples mutually victimized? A gender sensitive comparison. *Violence and Victims, 9*, 107–124.

Watson, V. M. (1989). Minorities and the legacy of anger. *APA Monitor, 20*(11), 30–31.

Weisinger, H. (1985). *The anger workout book.* New York: Quill.

Worell, J., & Remer, P. (1992). *Feminist perspectives in therapy: An empowerment model for women.* New York: Wiley.

■ ■ ■

8

Feminist Family Therapy With Families Affected by Disability

Brandon Hunt, PhD
Connie Matthews, PhD

There are several reasons why family therapists should have knowledge and awareness of the influence of disability on family functioning. First, all people, including people with disabilities, have families (whether family of origin or family of choice). Second, we live in an aging society, and older people have the highest incidence of disability. This is relevant for families because as people age, adult children and adult grandchildren become caregivers. Third, more people are surviving traumatic injuries and acquired disabilities as a result of advances in medical technology, rather than dying as a result of these injuries as they would have even 5 to 10 years ago. In addition, advances in assistive technology are helping people with disabilities to live more integrated and fulfilling lives, enabling them to function in their homes and communities rather than being confined to a nursing or personal care home. A fourth reason for having awareness of disability issues is alcohol and other drug (AOD) use and abuse. Substance abuse is a disability in and of itself, which can affect all members of the family. In addition, children may be born with disabilities as a result of addiction (e.g., children born with fetal alcohol syndrome), or people may acquire a disability as a result of AOD involvement (e.g., a gang member who is shot and acquires a spinal cord injury). For these reasons, family therapists need to have greater awareness and knowledge about the influence of disability on the family; however, a review of the family therapy literature and feminist therapy literature provides little information about disability.

Before a person can begin to work with people with disabilities within the context of feminist family therapy, it is important to have an understanding of what is meant by disability as well as an awareness of the cultural context of disability. There are many different definitions of disability, depending on who is defining it and for what purpose. The Americans With Disabilities Act (ADA)—created to end discrimination against people with disabilities in the areas of public transportation, public accommodations, telecommunications, and employment—defines a "person with a disability as . . . having a physical or mental impairment that substantially limits one or more major life activities" (ADA, 1990, as quoted in Brodwin, Parker, & DeLaGarza, 1996, p. 166), including breathing, speaking, hearing, walking, talking, learning, or performing self-care activities (LaPlante, 1997). For this chapter, the ADA definition of disability is used.

In general, disabilities can be grouped into four major categories: physical (e.g., multiple sclerosis, spinal cord injury), mental (e.g., schizophrenia, major depression), substance abuse (e.g., alcoholism), and developmental (e.g., mental retardation, learning disabilities). It is estimated that between 36 and 43 million people in the United States have a disability (LaPlante, 1997), but it is difficult to come up with a finite number because there is no one accepted definition of *disability*. Not every person who fits any of the various definitions of disability sees himself or herself as a person with a disability, and each person's experience with disability is diverse and individualized.

> Whether a particular physical condition is disabling changes with time and place, depending on such factors as social expectations, the state of technology and its availability to people in that condition, the educational system, architecture, attitudes toward physical appearance, and the pace of life. (Wendell, 1997, p. 264)

In addition, because of the prejudice and discrimination often experienced by people with disabilities, those who are able to "pass" often do, in the hopes that if the disability can be invisible they will not suffer the further debilitation of social stigma.

Several other definitions are relevant when discussing disability and rehabilitation. Although they are often used interchangeably, *handicap* and *disability* do not mean the same thing. *Handicap* refers to "restrictions attributable to social policy or barriers (structural or attitudinal), that limit fulfillment of roles or deny access to services and/or opportunities that are associated with full participation in society" (Maki & Riggar, 1997, pp. 8–9). *Handicapism* refers to discrimination and prejudice directed toward people with disabilities. Because we live in a society that is biased against and stigmatizes people with disabilities, all people, including people with disabilities, must become aware of their own handicapism before they can work to eradicate it or before they can work effectively with clients and families experiencing disability.

With respect to language, preference within the field of rehabilitation is to refer to the person first, rather than the disability (LaForge, 1991). For example, the preferred language is *a person with mental retardation* rather than a *mentally retarded person*, and *a person with schizophrenia* rather than *a schizophrenic*. Using language in this way reflects the disability as a part of the person, not the sole defining feature of a person. This attention to the use of language is quite consistent with feminist approaches to therapy, which stress the power dynamics involved in being the one who gets to name things. For example, Brown (1994) pointed out that "this power to name and define reality serves to deepen and exacerbate the power imbalance and inequities between therapist and client" (p. 138). Thus, it is essential that the feminist family therapist be aware of and sensitive to the language that people with disabilities use to define their own experience of themselves, of the disability, and of their world as a person with a disability.

History and Philosophy of Rehabilitation Counseling

Throughout history, and even today, attitudes toward people with disabilities have been influenced by a variety of factors. Safilias-Rothschild (1970, as cited in Havranek, 1991) identified the following factors:

> degree of a country's socioeconomic development and rate of unemployment; prevailing notions about the origin of poverty and unemployment and the role of the government; societal beliefs about the etiology of illness and degree of individual responsibility for the disability; the stigma attached to differ-

ent physical conditions; disability-connected factors such as visibility of illness, whether the illness is contagious, body part involved, degree of functional impairment, and degree of predictability of the course of the impairment; and effectiveness of public relations on the group's behalf. (p. 16)

The philosophy of rehabilitation, developed out of this historical context, is based on the following elements or beliefs. First, rehabilitation services should be designed and implemented that meet all of a person's needs—physical, mental, emotional, sexual, social, and spiritual. Second, people with disabilities should be empowered to make their own choices and decisions—no matter how limited their functioning may appear to be—to the degree they are able to and want to make such decisions and choices. Third, people with disabilities have the right and responsibility to be contributing members of their society. Fourth, rehabilitation focuses on a person's strengths and abilities, not functional limitations and deficits. Fifth, the environment should also be altered and improved to be more accommodating to people with disabilities rather than trying to adapt the person to the environment (G. Wright, 1980). In addition, B. A. Wright (1983, pp. xi–xvi) created 20 "value-laden beliefs and principles" for the field of rehabilitation, 3 of which seem particularly relevant to this topic:

1. The severity of a handicap can be increased or diminished by environmental conditions.
2. Issues of coping with and adjusting to a disability cannot be validly considered without examining reality problems in the social and physical environment.
3. In addition to the special problems of particular groups, rehabilitation clients commonly share certain problems by virtue of their disadvantaged and devalued position.

Although there have been people with disabilities throughout history, the field of rehabilitation as we know it today is a relatively new phenomenon. In the United States, rehabilitation grew out of federal government mandates. Because of cultural influences and expectations, men were primarily served by this early legislation. In addition, the laws were developed and enacted by men, primarily White men who did not have disabilities, so paternalism and government intervention were prevalent. This cultural context needs to be considered when examining how rehabilitation services are provided to this day. In recent decades, the focus has shifted from trying to change the person with the disability to working to alter the environment to accommodate the person with a disability, as well as eliminating societal barriers.

Similarities Between Rehabilitation and Feminism

There are a number of similarities between feminism (including feminist family therapy) and rehabilitation philosophy, in part because the disability civil rights movement of the 1970s and 1980s was influenced by the civil rights movements of women and people of color in the 1960s (Rubin & Roessler, 1995). In this section, we focus on four of these similarities: (a) the personal is political, (b) the role of power, (c) the influence of gender and disability status, and (d) the role of the counselor and the counseling relationship. Neither feminist family therapy nor rehabilitation counseling is a theory per se but a framework for viewing a situation. "Feminist family therapy is not a set of techniques, but a political and philosophical viewpoint which produces a therapeutic methodology by informing the questions the therapist asks and the understanding the therapist develops" (Goodrich, Rampage, Ellman, & Halstead, 1988, p. 21). As noted earlier, rehabilitation is also based on a philosophical and political point of view about people with disabilities.

The Personal Is Political

One important similarity between feminist family therapy and rehabilitation is the perspective that "the personal is political." This notion is an outgrowth of the consciousness-raising groups that were prominent in the early stages of the second wave of feminism in the United States (Enns, 1993). Women came together to share their experiences and, in the process, discovered that many of the personal difficulties they experienced were common to other women and could be traced more to inequities inherent in the current social structure than to personal inadequacies. Feminist therapy grew out of the awareness that individual problems are often reflective of social problems, specifically systematic oppression, and that the focus for therapy often belongs more on the external than the internal (Gilbert, 1980; Worell & Remer, 1992).

Feminist family therapy focuses on the interrelationship between the person, family, and society (Fish, 1989) as a source of change, as does rehabilitation. Feminist family therapy also views the person and the family as political (Pilalis & Anderton, 1986). Societal context, stigma, and expectations influence individuals and their families, whether they have a disability or not. Although rehabilitation does not use the language of the personal is political, political advocacy for people with disabilities is similar to this point of view. Part of the focus of rehabilitation is changing the environment and larger social structure to accommodate the person by eliminating architectural and attitudinal barriers and obstacles, rather than changing the person to fit into society. The sociopolitical model of disability "regards disability as a product of interactions between individual and environment by recognizing that the fundamental restrictions of a disability may be located in the surroundings that people encounter rather than within the disabled individual" (Hahn, 1988, p. 39).

Rehabilitation professionals acknowledge that accessibility issues and barriers are influenced by public policy, which is in turn influenced by societal assumptions, values, attitudes, and beliefs about people with disabilities. Although feminist family therapy and rehabilitation view the environment (including society) as creating problem situations for people, they also agree that part of the role of the therapist is to help clients and families take action on their own behalf. Both approaches consider anger at the social system to be appropriate, so they encourage using the energy from that anger as a means for empowerment and change.

In viewing the personal as political within the context of family therapy for people with disabilities, one must remember that

> families are interdependent and that a disability in one member affects all family members, that is, no one is exempt from the effects of a disability in the family. Furthermore, families are affected by institutions (schools, hospitals, clinics, etc.) that are removed from the family yet play an important role in the supportive structure that surrounds them. . . . And beyond the family and the institutions, there are major social–political forces that facilitate or hamper families' efforts on behalf of the person with the disability. Political action resulting in social policy decisions can add needed resources, take them away, or complicate access to resources by erecting barriers. (Hornby & Seligman, 1991, pp. 267–268)

The Role of Power

Although the focus is different, feminist family therapy and rehabilitation address the issue of individual power on a personal and societal level, because "both [are] based on the principle of equality of power" (Fowler, O'Rourke, Wadsworth, & Harper, 1992, p. 18). Feminist theory focuses on the inferior status of women (Fish, 1989; Goodrich et al., 1988), whereas rehabilitation focuses on the inferior status of people with disabilities. This is not to say that women and people with disabilities have the same level of power, or lack thereof, rather that they both address power as an important variable. Yet there seems to be a gap in the feminist and disability literature. A review of the feminist literature shows a significant lack of information and inclusion of women with disabilities, whereas the rehabilitation literature addresses issues that seem more relevant for men.

From a feminist perspective, men have power in society, and the role of feminist therapy is to redistribute power in a more equitable way. From a rehabilitation perspective, people without disabilities have the power. Because people with disabilities may not have the same abilities and physical similarities as people without disabilities, they have less power in society. This lack of power can be seen in instances in which people with disabilities may not be provided with employment opportunities or are institutionalized rather than given housing options in the community. Even within the disability community, there is a hierarchy of power—White men first, then men of color, followed by White women, and women of color. As Fine and Asch (1981) stated, "No doubt, disabled men too have to fight the stigmatized view of disabled people held by the nondisabled. They are nonetheless relatively advantaged in that they can observe and may aspire to the advantaged place of males in today's society" (p. 233).

Two important values in Western culture are the importance of personal appearance and autonomy. People with disabilities may not look like the idealized beauty portrayed by the media, and because of functional limitations, they may not be able to meet the societal expectations of independence. Because they do not meet these expectations, they may be stigmatized and shunned because they make other people uncomfortable. Often independence is seen as the ultimate goal of rehabilitation, but this is not always a possibility, or even a choice, for people with disabilities. Some people with disabilities may need to depend on others for help with activities of daily living, including dressing, eating, and transportation (Wendell, 1997). Others may view "dependence" as an essential part of their familial and cultural background and may not agree with or condone a view of total independence, especially if it is at the cost of a familial relationship. "The ultimate test for respect of autonomy can be found in the degree to which professional service providers are willing to honor the right of individuals to refuse treatments that service providers strongly believe are necessary for their welfare" (Gatens-Robinson & Rubin, 1995, p. 168).

Appearance and autonomy are key issues for feminists as well. Feminists have long struggled against the societal emphasis on appearance, especially for women. They recognize that it carries with it social controls that limit not only opportunity but also well-being. "It is not their appearance per se but the meaning that it holds for others and to each person in childhood, adolescence, and through-out life that shapes women and men" (Kaschak, 1992, p. 91). Those meanings for people with disabilities, as for women, usually pre-scribe diminished status, if not outright scorn, for those who do not meet society's standards. As in other areas, the issue of power arises as one looks more closely at who gets to set those standards and whom they benefit. The attendant effect on psychological well-being is frequently an issue addressed in therapy.

Autonomy is more complex. On the one hand, much of the femi-nist movement has been directed toward arguing against the soci-etal expectation of women's dependence on men. At the same time, some feminists, especially those working in the psychological arena, have questioned the very notion of total independence or autonomy as a value. Writers such as Carol Gilligan (1982), Jean Baker Miller (1986), and others (see, e.g., Jordan, Kaplan, Miller, Stiver, & Sur-rey, 1991) have suggested that women tend to be more relationship oriented compared with men and that this sense of connection to others is valuable. A goal for therapy then becomes reexamining one's values in this area and learning to maintain connection while minimizing the disempowering aspects of complete dependence. This seems especially relevant with respect to disability. Connec-tion might be vital for the survival of the person with the disability, but it need not necessarily be one-sided.

Influence of Gender and Disability Status

Another similarity is the role or influence of gender in feminist therapy and disability status in rehabilitation. Feminist family therapy focuses on the historical, social, political, and economic contexts of bias against women (Pilalis & Anderton, 1986). In rehabilitation, the focus is the historical, social, political, and economic contexts of bias against people with disabilities. Again, this is not to say that bias based on gender and bias based on disability are the same, only that for both groups people are discriminated or prejudiced against because of one quality or characteristic and that negative bias is solely based on societal stigma and conditioning. Therefore, women with disabilities are doubly stigmatized, and non-White or nonheterosexual women with disabilities face issues related to triple levels of stigma. With respect to the role of disability in a person's life, Fine and Asch (1981) stated:

> Being disabled is a characteristic sufficient to stereotype an individual. Disabled men and women are viewed, and often come to view themselves, as primarily disabled. Societal perceptions of disabled persons tend to be influenced entirely by the disability. Whether born disabled or having become disabled, the nondisabled world insists that disability is the predominant characteristic by which a person is labeled. (p. 237)

Related to the issues of gender and power, women and girls with disabilities are more likely to be physically and sexually abused than women and children who are not disabled (Abbott, 1994; Benefield & Head, 1984). Sexual abuse is not about having sex with an individual with a disability; it is about power and control. Furthermore, some women and girls acquire their disabilities as a result of family violence and sexual assault.

In many cultures, women with disabilities are not viewed as having a true illness or disabling condition. Instead, their behavior is seen as hypochondria or a cry for attention of some sort. Women with chronic illness face this issue frequently. Some disabling conditions are difficult to diagnose, and because we know more about male bodies and their functioning, many times women with disabilities are misdiagnosed or not diagnosed at all. For example, during the first decade of HIV disease, many women died of AIDS-related complications, although they were never diagnosed as having AIDS. The Centers for Disease Control and Prevention's previous definition focused on the symptoms men experience, so many women were not diagnosed, or even tested, to determine whether they were HIV-infected. Some agencies only provide services to people who have a diagnosis of AIDS, not just HIV infection, including housing, medical treatment, and access to free drug trials; therefore, women are adversely affected. In the case of drug trials, oftentimes women of "child-bearing years" (ages 16–55) are not included in drug trials because of concerns the women will become pregnant while taking the medication. This means that little is known about how drugs affect women, including possible consequences and side effects. A related example is treatment programs for alcohol and other drugs.

More programs are available for men than for women, and treatment programs are designed on the basis of what works with men (Abbott, 1994).

According to feminist theory, women are conditioned to be nurturing caretakers, responsible for caring for the emotional well-being of their partners and children, but women with disabilities are viewed as asexual beings who should not have children (Benefield & Head, 1984; Reinelt & Fried, 1993). Because a woman's other primary role is "sexual servicing of the male" (Burstow, 1992, p. 93), this creates a sense of rolelessness for women with disabilities (Fine & Asch, 1981). Given that a high percentage of men will leave their female partners if the partners become disabled (Disabled Women's Network, 1990, as cited in Burstow, 1992), this "sense" of rolelessness usually becomes a literal reality. Counselors working with families affected by disability need to be aware of the effect of long-standing societal myths about people with disabilities as parents, providers, and sexual partners on themselves, the families they counsel, and society at large.

Role of the Counselor and the Counseling Relationship

Both feminist therapy and rehabilitation counseling take an egalitarian approach to the counseling relationship. Federal legislation mandates the inclusion of clients in their own rehabilitation plan (Rubin & Roessler, 1995). To maintain equity in the counseling relationship, rehabilitation counselors and feminist family therapists view clients with respect and value them as partners in the process. Although the counselor or therapist is the person with training and experience, there is a belief that clients know what is best for themselves and counselors are viewed as helpers in the process. In feminist family therapy, the therapist is "accountable" to the family, is aware of her or his own values and power within the relationship, and is willing to discuss these elements (Pilalis & Anderton, 1986).

Both feminist family therapy and rehabilitation counseling are action oriented. In feminist family therapy, the "client is encouraged not only to develop insights about her role in maintaining the familial and societal contexts of which she is a part, but also to take responsibility for changing them" (Ault-Riche, 1986, p. 2). The goal to work toward is "change, not adjustment; social change, family change, individual change, with intent to transform the social relations which define men's and women' s existence" (Goodrich et al., 1988, p. 12). The same could be said for rehabilitation counseling.

It is important for professionals who work with people with disabilities and their families to assess their own attitudes, biases, beliefs, values, and stereotypes about disability. All people—including people with disabilities themselves— have the potential to have negative attitudes toward people with disabilities because we are socialized in a society that discriminates against people with disabilities. In addition, people with disabilities may be open and accepting of some disability groups while biased against others. "In sum, feminist and rehabilitation philosophies generally agree on an abstract level regarding the value of [an] individual's worth, the empowerment of an individual to direct the course of her [or his] life, and the potential power of an individual's environment to effect that experience" (Fowler et al., 1992, p. 16).

Counseling Strategies and Suggestions

When working with a family in which one or more people in the family have a disability, there are a number of counseling strategies and suggestions that may be helpful. The first has to do with the comfort level of the feminist family therapist in dealing with the disability itself. Practical strategies are important. The feminist family therapist may need to rearrange her or his office or meet in an accessible location depending on the person's disabilities, for example, with a person who uses a wheelchair. If this is the case, the therapist should ask the person and family members the most effective way to arrange things. Other people may need to rearrange furniture because of a visual impairment (e.g., to avoid glare or painful light in their eyes) or so they can see everyone who is speaking if they have a hearing impairment. Remembering to rearrange furniture before the family arrives can be an important part of obtaining and maintaining trust and rapport in the therapist–client relationship. It is a way to acknowledge that the disability exists and that the therapist is aware of what it means to the family.

Another useful strategy is to talk directly to the person with the disability, even if she or he has a communication disorder. If the person uses an interpreter, the feminist family therapist should still face the client when speaking. Talking only to family members or interpreters disempowers the person with a disability. If the therapist does not know about the disability or is unsure how to respond to the client and the family, there are several options. The first is to explain to the client and the family that the therapist's knowledge is limited and that he or she would like them to talk about what the disability means to each of them. Feminist family therapists should not expect the family to automatically educate them about the disability, and they should be careful not to make the person with the disability the spokesperson for all people with that particular disability. Also, the feminist family therapist should let the family know that he or she will do research and learn more about the disability before the next session. After meeting with the family, the therapist may want to contact support groups or agencies that focus on the particular disability, for example, the Multiple Sclerosis Society or the American Cancer Society. Using the World Wide Web is another way to gather information, because many groups now have web pages that provide a wide variety of information about the disability. It is also important for feminist family therapists to be aware of local organizations to which they might want to refer the client and family for additional information and services. A third option is to receive supervision or to consult with a professional who has knowledge about the disability and what it might mean for the client and his or her family.

When the therapist first meets with a family, it is important to assess the significance and relevance of the disability in terms of why the family has come in for therapy. Feminist family therapists do not assume that every family comes to counseling for issues related to the disability, but they do not assume the opposite either. As part of the initial assessment, Power and Dell Orto (1986, p. 42) suggested that family counselors explore the following areas with respect to disability issues:

1. What is the unique composition of the family, and what are the strengths and pitfalls inherent in that structure that would influence the client's rehabilitation?
2. What has the family done so far to respond to the disability or illness?
3. What information does the family have about the disability or illness condition, and with this knowledge, what expectations does the family have for their disabled family member?
4. What services does the family need, such as financial, respite care, or family counseling?

Communication style and patterns are another important area to assess. How is the disability discussed within the family, outside of the family, and by different members? Do they use humor, denial, or positive references only? Also, how able are family members to locate and use community resources and to respond to the needs of the family member with a disability? If the disability is related to the reason why the family came in for counseling, it is useful to ask each person what the disability means to her or him as a group and individually. The feminist family therapist should not focus only on the affective level (although it is important) but should also ask members what the disability means to them on a practical, day-to-day basis. What are their thoughts and feelings about the disability itself, as well as the person with the disability and how their lives are affected because of it? It is essential for each person to accept responsibility for his or her own feelings and actions with regard to the disability.

When counseling a person with a disability, the feminist family therapist must keep age, gender, ethnicity, socioeconomic status, and other variables in mind. Each of these elements influences the person's perception of what having a disability means to him or her. For example, a 5-year-old poor Black girl may have a very different experience with disability than a 45-year-old poor White woman. Age of onset, type of disability, and how the disability was acquired are also influencing factors. In addition, functional limitations, compensation skills, and the person's self-perception affect how the person functions within the context of his or her disability. Disabilities may be visible or invisible, each of which presents its own challenges for people with disabilities and their families. When working with a family in which one or more members have a disability, the therapist must consider these factors for each person, as well as the synergistic effect of each factor.

Disability may cause a number of changes in the family, including economic changes, social changes, and emotional changes (Sutton, 1985). Families of people with disabilities may experience high levels of stress, financial hardships, and stigmatization. They may also worry that the disability may happen to them (especially siblings). Depending on the disability, there may be less outside socialization and less flexible routines, and the families may have more medical and hospital care and experiences. Making referrals to formal and informal support groups and organizations may benefit the family.

Rather than follow the medical model inherent in rehabilitation, feminist family therapists look at a family's strengths as opposed to pathology or dysfunction. They assess whether family members are able to listen to one another as well as to professionals. They look for a shared perception of reality within the family. This does not mean that everyone has to agree to the same story, only that they are aware of the views and perspectives of other family members. Feminist family therapists also consider whether family members have the ability and willingness to shift roles and responsibilities as needed. The shifting of roles and responsibilities is not based on gender role stereotypes but on the family's needs and interests.

Possible "negative" reactions from family members may include "overprotection, encouragement of dependency, neglect, avoidance of future planning, denial of diagnosis, excessive and inappropriate demands, and punitive action toward the family member with a disability" (Versluys, 1980, p. 59). These reactions may serve a purpose within the family system and should not automatically be assumed to be negative or pathological. They may be coping strategies or the only way the family knows how to react in such a situation. They may also be responses to environmental pressures such as discrimination, harassment, stigma, or other active forms of prejudice. As part of the process, it is important for feminist family therapists to determine the extent to which these conditions actually exist, or whether the family is functioning in a way contrary to how the therapist thinks they should be, and, therefore, the behavior is viewed as pathological or negative. Looking to the family's strengths and how they handled previous traumatic or crisis situations is one way to work through negative or dysfunctional responses to disability.

From a family systems perspective, awareness of the power of homeostasis both within the family and in the larger social system and the ways that it may undermine the counseling process is critical. Making family members aware of homeostasis and the significance of power in the system is one way to work with these two strong forces. Educating family members to serve as advocates for themselves and the person with a disability empowers each person to make choices and decisions that are informed and well thought out. Whereas traditional approaches to counseling and therapy often place the counselor in the role of expert, feminist therapy stresses a more egalitarian approach. Recognizing that in many situations knowledge is power, feminist therapists often strive to provide clients with the information necessary to reclaim their personal power. This involves teaching clients about different kinds of power and the ways in which power is differentially distributed in society, as well as helping them to use their own power to influence the course of their lives.

Regardless of when, how, or why the disability occurred, there are a number of practical skills and abilities that are useful for families. To learn effective ways to adapt to change, the person with the disability and his or her family can try possible training and intervention strategies, including time management, behavior management, stress management, and decision-making and problem-solving training. Families can also be taught how to contact other families and resource groups for support and education purposes, for example, how to address social stigma when they are in public. In addition, families should be informed of possible respite care options. Respite care involves volunteers or paid staff who provide care for the person with a disability while the primary caretaker leaves to take care of other issues. Some families may not want to use respite care but they, and the therapist, need to be aware of caregiver burnout. It is useful to check out whether people will not use respite care because of role expectations and stereotypes within and outside of the family, especially as related to gender and power.

Two other important skills to teach families are communication and negotiation skills, particularly with medical and rehabilitation personnel. This can be viewed as similar to self-advocacy. Family members and the person with the disability may need to interact with and gain information from a wide variety of medical personnel, insurance providers, and government agencies (including social services and schools) that maintain sexism and handicapism, so communication, assertiveness, and self-advocacy skills are necessary tools. Because of previous experiences, family members may have little trust in helping professionals (especially medical personnel), which could negatively affect the therapy relationship. Openly discussing previous experiences is one way to work through this issue. Transition times can be especially stressful for families affected by disability (Cooley & Moeschler, 1993). Developmental milestones and rituals may be different, delayed, or bypassed (e.g., driver's license and people who are visually impaired) because of the disability. Moving to a new area may mean finding all new services, which can be stressful. Attention to grief reactions that may be reactivated during transition times is important.

Mary and Her Family

Mary is a 42-year-old mother of three children: a 17-year-old son, Rich, and two daughters, Casey, age 14, and Jessie, age 13. Jessie's school counselor referred the family for counseling after Jessie, traditionally a strong and engaging student, began having problems in school. When a series of school-based interventions were unsuccessful, the school counselor suspected the academic problems were manifestations of what she knew to be a difficult family situation.

As a result of an automobile accident 3 years ago, Mary is paralyzed from the waist down and uses a wheelchair. She was hospitalized for 3 months immediately after the accident. Prior to the accident, she and her husband, Rick, had a marriage that was without tension but also without passion. For the most part, Mary and Rick led their own lives, although both were devoted to the children and involved in many family activities. Rick was clearly the head of the family and made all of the major decisions. About 1 year ago, Rick left the family. Initially, Rick saw the children regularly; however, he has substantially reduced his time with them during the past 6 months since he began seeing another woman. His explanation for his lack of involvement is that their mother needs them at home and he does not want to take them away from her.

Mary returned to her job following her stay in the hospital but has not seen the regular promotions she was receiving prior to her accident. Indeed, she has felt somewhat stalled at work since her return. Although Mary is in a professional position, the family finances have suffered considerably since Rick's departure.

Rich's response to his mother's accident has been to be very protective. In fact, all of the children rallied to support her. Rich immediately began doing extra work around the house and took care of his sisters while his father made frequent trips to the hospital. Since his father left the family, Rich has stepped into more of a paternal role with both his sisters and his mother. Rich contributes most of the money from his part-time job to help the family with the financial hardship created when his father left. He has recently taken to making family decisions on his own, which has caused tension within the family. Jessie and Casey have assumed more of the responsibility for family meals and other household chores. Occasionally, they also baby-sit for several neighbors and have offered their baby-sitting money to pay the family's bills.

There are a number of factors that the feminist family therapist would consider when working with this family. To begin with, the feminist family therapist would acknowledge that Mary is not the only one who has suffered from her accident. In their rush to support their mother, it is probable that the children have not had an opportunity to address the ways in which they too have suffered. This suffering is likely to include a deteriorating relationship with their father. The feminist family therapist would help the family sort out what factors are directly related to the disability and which are being attributed to the disability but may be separate. Likewise, the feminist family therapist would encourage Mary to talk about what it is like for her to feel that she has to be cared for by her children. It may be appropriate for both Mary and her children to receive some education about Mary's disability with respect to both capabilities and limitations.

The feminist family therapist would address family roles, especially with respect to gender and gender role stereotypes. There appear to be a number of factors at work regarding how the family has adapted to Mary having a disability and the marital separation. Rich seems to have appointed himself man of the family in his father's absence, and this role is exacerbated by his mother's disability. At the same time, the other family members have willingly allowed him this role, at least until very recently. Again, exploring Rich's role, as well as other family members' roles, within the context of gender stereotypes and understanding of and attitudes toward Mary's disability would be a focus for the feminist family therapist. Differentials in power would also be addressed.

Developmental factors involved with adolescence compound the family's difficulties, especially as Rich struggles to become an adult in general and an adult male in particular. Casey and Jessie are also in adolescence and facing all of society's messages about what it means to be young women. Feminist family therapists would explore the meaning of these messages with the family and help them understand their gendered context. Appropriate alternative messages not seeped in patriarchal assumptions would be offered.

The financial situation presents another issue, which will need exploration. All family members would be given the opportunity to talk about the impact of the financial change for them. Mary's work situation would be included in this exploration. Why have the promotions stopped? Had Mary already reached her maximum potential? Is discrimination part of what is occurring? If so, is this related to gender (i.e., has she reached the glass ceiling) or disability or both? To what extent, if any, has Mary limited herself on the basis of her own notions of what is and is not possible with her disability? Is Mary experiencing internalized handicapism? Helping Mary to accurately assess her work situation and to act as an advocate on her own behalf may be appropriate.

In summary, the feminist family therapist would encourage this family to explore their concerns within the larger social context, emphasizing options beyond rigid gender role stereotypes. Power issues would be examined, including how decisions are made in the family and how labor is divided. Family members would be challenged to develop insight into their roles in maintaining oppressive contexts, whether related to sexism or handicapism, and to take responsibility for changing them. This exploration would take place within an egalitarian, collaborative relationship.

Conclusion

Despite many overlaps in philosophy and approach, feminist family therapy and rehabilitation counseling have not traditionally been considered together. The feminist family therapy literature has largely ignored issues related to disability of one or more family members. Likewise, the rehabilitation literature has failed to adequately address factors related to gender and power in adapting to or accommodating disability. This connection must be made. Disability can affect any family at any time, and when it does, family therapists need to be able to effectively address the impact that it has on all family members and on the family as a unit. Often the adjustments that must occur are further complicated by gender role expectations within the family and in society at large. As this chapter suggests, there are many areas in which feminist family therapy and rehabilitation counseling share common approaches. These include (a) attention to the role of the social context in understanding client/family problems; (b) an orientation toward action; (c) an effort to make the counseling relationship egalitarian and to actively involve the family in the process; (d) awareness of the role of power in the counseling relationship, the family, and society; and (e) a commitment to avoid "blaming the victim" for problems stemming from the oppression faced by women and people with disabilities. It should, therefore, be possible and advisable to bring a feminist family therapy approach to rehabilitation counseling when working within the context of family therapy.

References

Abbott, A. A. (1994). A feminist approach to substance abuse treatment and service delivery. *Social Work in Health Care, 19*(3–4), 67–83.

Ault-Riche, M. (1986). A feminist critique of five schools of family therapy. In M. Ault-Riche (Ed.), *Women and family therapy* (pp. 1–23). Rockville, MD: Aspen.

Benefield, L., & Head, D. W. (1984). Discrimination and disabled women. *Humanistic Education and Development, 23*(2), 60–68.

Brodwin, M., Parker, R. M., & DeLaGarza, D. (1996). Disability and accommodation. In E. M. Szymanski & R. M. Parker (Eds.), *Work and disability: Issues and strategies in career development and job placement* (pp. 165–207). Austin, TX: Pro-Ed.

Brown, L. S. (1994). *Subversive dialogues.* New York: Basic Books.

Burstow, B. (1992). *Radical feminist therapy: Working in the context of violence.* Newbury Park, CA: Sage.

Cooley, W. C., & Moeschler, J. B. (1993). Counseling in the health care relationship. In G. H. S. Singer & L. E. Powers (Eds.), *Families, disability, and empowerment: Active coping, skills and strategies for family interventions* (pp. 155–174). Baltimore: Paul H. Brooks.

Enns, C. Z. (1993). Twenty years of feminist counseling and therapy: From naming biases to implementing multifaceted practice. *The Counseling Psychologist, 21,* 3–87.

Fine, M., & Asch, A. (1981). Disabled women: Sexism without the pedestal. *Journal of Sociology and Social Welfare, 8,* 233–248.

Fish, L. S. (1989). Comparing structural, strategic, and feminist-informed family therapies: Two Delphi studies. *American Journal of Family Therapy, 17,* 303–314.

Fowler, C., O'Rourke, B., Wadsworth, J., & Harper, D. (1992). Disability and feminism: Models for counselor exploration of personal values and beliefs. *Journal of Applied Rehabilitation Counseling, 23*(4), 14–19.

Gatens-Robinson, E., & Rubin, S. E. (1995). Societal values and ethical commitments that influence rehabilitation service delivery behavior. In S. E. Rubin & R. T. Roessler (Eds.), *Foundation of the vocational rehabilitation process* (4th ed., pp. 157–174). Austin, TX: Pro-Ed.

Gilbert, L. A. (1980). Feminist therapy. In A. M. Brodsky & R. Hare-Mustin (Eds.), *Women and psychotherapy: An assessment of research and practice* (pp. 245–265). New York: Guilford Press.

Gilligan, C. (1982). *In a different voice.* Cambridge, MA: Harvard University Press.

Goodrich, T. J., Rampage, C., Ellman, B., & Halstead, K. (1988). *Feminist family therapy: A casebook.* New York: Norton.

Hahn, H. (1988). The politics of physical differences: Disability and discrimination. *Journal of Social Issues, 44*(1), 39–47.

Havranek, J. E. (1991). The social and individual costs of negative attitudes toward persons with disabilities. *Journal of Applied Rehabilitation Counseling, 22*(1), 15–21.

Hornby, G., & Seligman, M. (1991). Disability and the family: Current status and future developments. *Counseling Psychology Quarterly, 4,* 267–271.

Jordan, J. V., Kaplan, A. G., Miller, J. B., Stiver, I. P., & Surrey, J. L. (Eds.). (1991). *Women's growth in connection: Writings from the Stone Center.* New York: Guilford Press.

Kaschak, E. (1992). *Engendered lives.* New York: Basic Books.

LaForge, J. (1991). Preferred language practice in professional rehabilitation journals. *Journal of Rehabilitation, 57*(1), 49–51.

LaPlante, M. P. (1997, June). *How many Americans have a disability?* [On-line]. Available: dsc.ucsf.edu/abs/ab5.html.

Maki, D. R., & Riggar, T. F. (1997). *Rehabilitation counseling: Profession and practice.* New York: Springer.

Miller, J. B. (1986). *Toward a new psychology of women.* Boston: Beacon Press.

Pilalis, J., & Anderton, J. (1986). Feminism and family therapy—a possible meeting point. *Journal of Family Therapy, 8,* 99–114.

Power, P. W., & Dell Orto, A. E. (1986). Families, illness and disability: The roles of the rehabilitation counselor. *Journal of Applied Rehabilitation Counseling,17*(2), 41–44.

Reinelt, C., & Fried, M. (1993). "I am this child's mother": A feminist perspective on mothering with a disability. In M. Nagler (Ed.), *Perspectives on disability* (2nd ed., pp. 195–202). Palo Alto, CA: Health Markets Research.

Rubin, S. E., & Roessler, R. T. (Eds.). (1995). *Foundation of the vocational rehabilitation process* (4th ed.). Austin, TX: Pro-Ed.

Sutton, J. (1985). The need for family involvement in client rehabilitation. *Journal of Applied Rehabilitation Counseling, 16*(1), 42–45.

Versluys, H. P. (1980). Physical rehabilitation and family dynamics. *Rehabilitation Literature, 41*(3–4), 58–66.

Wendell, S. (1997). Toward a feminist theory of disability. In L. J. Davis (Ed.), *The disability studies reader* (pp. 260–278). New York: Routledge.

Worell, I., & Remer, P. (1992). *Feminist perspectives in therapy: An empowerment model for women.* New York: Wiley.

Wright, B. A. (1983). *Physical disability—a psychosocial approach* (2nd ed.). Philadelphia: Harper & Row.

Wright, G. (1980). *Total rehabilitation.* Boston: Little, Brown.

■ ■ ■

9

A Feminist Perspective on Sexuality Issues in Family Therapy

Victoria A. Foster, PhD

Sexual socialization of children within the family has warranted greater attention in recent years (e.g., Barnett, Papini, & Gbur, 1991; Benshoff & Alexander, 1993; Maddock, 1990; Santelli & Beilenson, 1992). Diverse theoretical approaches to this expanding and eclectic field of practice have increased understanding and clarity about the impact of sexuality on the individual's and the family's overall sense of well-being. Simultaneously, potentially serious threats related to sexual behavior include sexually transmitted diseases, especially HIV, and the psychological, educational, and economic consequences of early pregnancy and sexual victimization. Inadequate sex education contributes to serious social problems and family dysfunction (Benshoff & Alexander, 1993). These risks combine to raise concern about the process and outcomes of sexual socialization and education from generation to generation.

The feminist critique of family therapy has resulted in a dramatic increase in the attention given to gender, sex roles, race, culture, and power in family theory and practice (Avis, 1988; Nichols & Schwartz, 1998). This critique has yet to address the role of sexual-

ity, including both gender and eroticism, as an inherent and fundamental component in family processes. Sexuality as a focus of the
therapeutic conversation in family counseling has been generally
ignored, except when specific sexual problems are identified, such
as sexual abuse or sexual dysfunction (MacKinnon & Miller, 1985;
Maddock, 1990). More recently, particular attention regarding sexuality is disproportionately assigned to African American underprivi-
leged girls, about whom contraception practices and rates of
premarital pregnancy are the central concerns (Fine & Macpherson,
1992).

Recent research indicates that the highest content priority in
sexuality courses reported in a survey of counselor education programs was that of sexual dysfunctions (Gray, House, & Eicken,
1996). The absence of an emphasis on sexual developmental issues throughout the life span and the focus on sexual performance
perpetuate the dominant cultural model of sexuality as the prov-
ince of adults. There is a special emphasis on a normative model
of functioning based on the achievement of sexual intercourse and
orgasm with a procreative definition of sex (Gray et al., 1996; Tiefer,
1996a, 1996b). Through the therapeutic isolation of sexuality from
the totality of human experience, it is objectified and isolated from
sociopolitical and cultural realities. The purpose of this chapter is
to provide a feminist analysis of family context and sexuality with
an awareness of the restrictive and constitutive dichotomies of
gender and to make recommendations for clinical practice in family sexuality.

Feminist Explorations of Sexuality

Feminist theory (and its application to family therapy) has argued that the social world is constructed on a premise of male superiority; that is, gender and the power asymmetries predicated on
gender are the foundations on which human relationships are organized (Fine, 1992). Furthermore, gender "braids with social class,
race/ethnicity, age, disability (or not) and sexual orientation as well
as social context to produce socially and historically constituted
subjectivities" (Fine, 1992, p. 3). Sexual behavior and feelings en-
compass all the contradictions of these power relations; thus, the
realities of sexual expectations and experiences throughout the life
cycle are constructed realities that are limited and controlled by
the patriarchal power structure. Even the biological facts of sexuality must be expressed as a social experience (Ross & Rapp, 1983).

This social structuring of sexuality is enacted within the family, the diverse elements of the community, and the larger culture. The impact of the family on the sexuality of its members reflects the social layers in which it is embedded and the specific characteristics of the family structure itself.

Feminist approaches to sexuality identify sex as a construct, historically and culturally determined and constituted in specific social practices (Rubin, 1984; Tiefer, 1996a, 1996b). Sexuality is seen as a fundamental dimension that organizes family experience, and thus, it is integral to the political struggle against the patriarchal structure through the development of sexual theory and practice. Such theory and practice embody questions about differentiation in the "sexual sphere" (Vance, 1984, p. 2), the nature of male and female sexuality, the effects of oppression on female sexuality, the relationship between sex and gender, and how race, class, ethnicity, and religion affect the experience and perception of sexuality (Almeida, Woods, Messineo, Font, & Heer, 1994; Vance, 1984). Through the institution of marriage and the maintenance of a double standard of sexual morality for men and women, female sexuality has been restricted to those areas sanctioned by U.S. culture: traditional heterosexual marriage and the nuclear family. Outside those boundaries, female sexuality is pathologized or condemned (Echols, 1984; Hare-Mustin, 1998).

In recent decades, however, political and technological changes have transformed the sexual landscape; the link between reproduction and sexuality is no longer absolute, and changes in family structure, behavioral norms, and demographics have altered social systems (Maddock, 1990, 1997; Vance & Pollis, 1990). The social and personal meanings of sexual identity and sexual behavior have varied historically. Current explorations of female sexual desire and expression have sought to expand the opportunities for women to move beyond the restrictions of the culture; to give voice to the complexity of relationships, behaviors, and desires that are present in people's daily lives; and to explore the distinctions between gender and erotic desire (Tolman, 1991, 1994). Nonetheless, sexuality issues, most notably abortion and homosexuality, remain among the most politically charged and carry immense symbolic weight (Johnson & Keren, 1998; Rubin, 1984). Attempts to restrict sexuality to the traditionally sanctioned areas are reminders of the simultaneous elements of power and danger posed by sexuality in our culture. Efforts to close down the conversation about sexuality from a feminist perspective are apparent but should be resisted:

We need to develop a feminist understanding of sexuality which
is not predicated on denial and repression, but which acknowledges the complexities and ambiguities of sexuality. Above all,
we should admit that we know far too little about sexuality to
embark upon a crusade to circumscribe it. Rather than fore-
close on sexuality we should identify what conditions will best
afford women sexual autonomy, safety, and pleasure and work
towards their realization. (Echols, 1984, p. 66)

What is clear is the need for research and practice that would
transform the epistemology of sexuality itself. The basis of our
understanding of sexuality has been predicated on social constructs
of gender, race, and power that have excluded all but privileged,
predominantly male voices and organized sexual behavior into
polarities of "good" (normal and natural) or "bad" (abnormal and
unnatural) behaviors. The notion of a single ideal norm-based sexuality inherent in a variety of disciplines assumes there exists some
natural sexuality underneath the socialization, the dominant culture, and the individual learning, if only it could be uncovered or
made apparent (Tiefer, 1996a, 1996b). Such reductionism must be
challenged and replaced with multifaceted approaches to sex research, education, and therapeutic practices that are collaborative
and interdisciplinary. A feminist agenda on sexuality promotes the
opportunity for women to define themselves, instead of having their
sexual identity defined by the dominant patriarchal culture. A social reconstruction of sexual identity simultaneously presents the
opportunity for men to renegotiate their own sexuality. Such rene-
gotiation and reconstruction would have a significant impact on
the family by altering sex roles, challenging cultural imperatives,
and expanding the opportunities for family members to construct
their lives and futures through critical discourse, reflection, and
affirmation.

Family Influences on Sexuality

The family represents the starting point of individual learning
about sexuality (Maddock, 1983, 1990). The politics and meaning
of gender are articulated through the family discourse (or silence)
on sexuality. In explicit and implicit communication through modeling, patterns of interaction, and consequences, the family articulates what forms of physical expression are acceptable for whom,
what sexual orientations are normal, who constitutes acceptable

sexual partners, and what kinds of relationships are expected and allowable.

The family serves as the conduit through which cultural socialization is embodied and transmitted to its members. Research findings for the last 20 years have generally noted that parents initiate children's education about sexuality in the first few months of life by laying the foundation for gender identity, gender-appropriate behaviors, and moral values (Calderone, 1984; Schnarch, 1991). Parents play an important role in the sexualization of their children, not only through direct sexual instruction but also through indirect sexual communications within the family.

According to Calderone (1984), sexuality is shaped by family and culture through explicit and implicit messages that define gender identity, gender role, and eroticism. Schnarch (1991) stated that "eroticism is one of the most powerful driving forces behind family dynamics and individual behavior—and one of the most denied" (p. 314). Much of the dissemination of sexual information is done inadvertently by parents and family members who may be unaware of the attitudinal messages they are presenting. The literature on the impact of the family on the sexuality of children has focused primarily on the role of parents in preventing or delaying premarital sexual intercourse or on the influence of family interaction patterns on sexual attitudes and behaviors, with an emphasis on contraception (Maddock, 1990). The central focus is on those factors that impact the likelihood of adolescent girls becoming pregnant outside of marriage.

Little of the research on sexuality and the family addresses the role of gender, race, culture, and power in assessing the family's influence on the sexual feelings, thoughts, and practices of its members. Racial and ethnic minorities are among the most sexually oppressed populations in U.S. culture; their sexual needs are distorted, suppressed, or made invisible (Almeida et al., 1994; Christensen, 1988). The highest rates of sexually transmitted diseases and pregnancy occur in younger adolescent girls, inner-city youths, and ethnic minority teens, indicating the significance of social and political factors in determining high risk for potentially severe health problems related to sexual activity (Yarber & Parrillo, 1992). A critical analysis of the factors of gender, race, class, and socioeconomic status is needed to more clearly understand sexuality in the family and cultural context. Most importantly, we must acknowledge how little we know about the actual experience of sexuality in the family context through the voices of mothers and fathers, daughters and sons, grandparents, aunts, uncles, and other extended family members who could describe their shared and individual realities with authenticity and complexity.

What have been emphasized in the research are variables that may control sexuality, especially the sexuality of adolescent girls. Without diminishing the risks of sexual behavior in the era of HIV and AIDS, it should be possible to explore the sexuality of adolescents and adults beyond the discourse promoted by the dominant culture. According to Fine (1992), four themes dominate the national discourse on sexuality and sex education. The first, sexuality as violence, views adolescent sexuality in particular as dangerous, coercive, and potentially harmful. Such a view presumes that silencing the discourse on sexuality will prevent sexual behavior. The second discourse, sexuality as victimization, portrays young women and, increasingly, young men (especially homosexual men) as potentially vulnerable to male predators. To protect themselves from becoming victims, sex is equated with resistance and defense against pregnancy, sexually transmitted diseases, and manipulation. The third discourse equates sexuality with an issue of individual morality. In this discourse, sexual values are acceptable and decision making is encouraged so long as the result is premarital abstinence. Morality is equated with family values, chastity, and self-control; outside this value system lie temptation and moral decay. The fourth discourse is the discourse of desire, the "naming of desire, pleasure, or sexual entitlement, particularly for females" (Fine, 1992, p. 35), that contradicts the dominant conversation surrounding sexuality. When it is spoken, according to Fine, there are always the reminders of the consequences of sexuality, couched in negative or problematic terms. A feminist approach to this discourse of desire constructs sexual meanings out of personal social contexts, that illuminate the experiences, needs, and limits of adolescents and adults. From a feminist perspective, sexuality and eroticism are "simultaneously personal, cultural, political, and social" (Webster, 1984, p. 391) and best understood in the context of personal, family, and social patterns (Almeida, Woods, Messineo, & Font, 1998; Hof & Berman, 1986).

Another significant finding throughout the literature is the limited nature of communication within the family related to sexuality topics at large. Studies have indicated that parents are unwilling or unable to effectively discuss comprehensive sexual topics with their children (Benshoff & Alexander, 1993; Santelli & Beilenson, 1992). Contemporary sexuality remains narrowly defined according to a complex interplay of gender and power that names what is acceptable and what is forbidden according to the contradictory needs of the dominant culture. The family system functions as a microcosm of the patriarchal culture in which it is embedded and thus discourages understanding and exploration of sensual pleasure and sexual identity. This cycle of sexual silences and discomfort must be interrupted to facilitate healthy sexual development.

Family Therapy and Sexuality

The feminist critique of traditional family therapy has challenged its reinforcement of stereotypical sex roles, including socially sanctioned expressions of sexuality, assumptions of normalcy of heterosexuality, and the "inevitability of male dominance" (Avis, 1988, p. 26). Most of the literature on sexuality issues in the family is focused on the integration of sex therapy into marriage work related to sexual dysfunctions or problems of intimacy in the couple relationship or on the sex education of children (Benshoff & Alexander, 1993; Maddock, 1990). Other work on family sexuality is more specific to problems of incest, sexual abuse, and family influence on sexual deviance. Generally, sexuality has been isolated from its construction within the larger culture. Surprisingly little scholarship was found regarding sexuality as an important organizing construct for family dynamics or as a positive component of family development.

Maddock (1983, 1990) offered some comprehensive work in this area and proposed a complex model of family sexuality to serve as a basis for research and to provide guidelines for clinical practice. The model includes four primary existential dimensions of family life: systemic, developmental, historical, and sexual. Each of these dimensions is seen to be in balance or in dialectical relationship with the others, thus creating an ecosystem of ongoing transformation among the embedded subsystems to maintain the homeostasis or integrity of the larger system. In the context of these interrelated family systems dimensions, Maddock (1983, pp. 6–12) articulated the following propositions:

1. Family sexual experience is pervasive and functional rather than isolated and aberrant.
2. Because the family unit consists of sexual persons, it represents the social meanings of femaleness and maleness to its members.
3. Differentiation of sex roles within the family system is a significant factor influencing interaction patterns and communication sequences between family members.

4. The family system organizes and expresses the embodiment of its members.
5. The nature and extent of sexual interaction among family members are largely a function of distance-regulating mechanisms in the family system and its social environment.
6. Sexual aspects of family experience are complexly related to other aspects of experience within the family system.
7. The course of various stages in the family life cycle is strongly influenced by significant events in the individual psychosexual development of family members; conversely, patterns of psychosexual development of individual members are strongly influenced by qualities of corresponding stages in the family life cycle.
8. Because the family is a highly "open" system, its sexual meanings and accompanying behavior patterns are mutually interactive with elements in its cultural–historic environment.

Maddock's (1983) model moved the focus on family sexuality beyond a problem-centered stance to a positive and integrative framework. Sexuality is depathologized and seen as a normal and essential element of psychological and biological family life. Sexually healthy families are those that maintain the dialectic of transformation among the needs of their members and the larger family system as a whole. With regard to sexuality, balanced interdependence of genders, boundaries, and communication patterns (both verbal and nonverbal), as well as shared sexual values, meanings, and beliefs within the family, would permit individual decision making and personal sexual expression. There is no mention of family configuration, although much of the model could be applicable to different family types. Implicitly, the model is descriptive of and oriented to White, dual-parent, intact nuclear families. No ethnic, class, racial, or cultural issues are addressed.

The dialectic of transformation in the balancing of needs both within the family system and between the family and the related subsystems within which it resides is viewed apolitically; that is, the question of unequal power in the family between gender and generation is not addressed. This systemic premise of neutrality emphasizes that all parts of the system contribute equally to family functioning. As noted by Avis (1988), differences in power and influence that directly affect sexual identity and sex role socialization are rendered "totally invisible" (p. 17). The feminist perspective affirms gender not as a dimension of sexuality but as a "fundamental category of human existence, and power (and gender related power differences) as a basic dimension in marital family relationships" (Avis, 1988, p. 26). MacKinnon and Miller (1985) stated that issues of social, economic, and political power inequities must be specifically addressed in family therapy to address the contextual realities of family life, including sexuality. Furthermore, recognizing the interactions of race, gender, and class and their relationship to power is essential to understanding the politics of sexuality in the family and in the larger culture in which the family resides.

Some feminists have suggested that the systems approach to family therapy and family conceptualization must undergo significant transformation before it will adequately address the complexity of oppression and domination represented in the family system and perpetuated by the larger patriarchal culture (Lerner, 1987). In terms of family sexuality, power must be the focus of attention in exploring the attitudes, beliefs, and values that are prevalent within the family and the influence of these frameworks on sexual identity, sexual behavior, and the sexual development of each family member. Knowledge that children and adolescents obtain directly and indirectly about sexuality occurs in the context of the frameworks that have been provided by their families (Walters & Walters, 1983). If families perpetuate the sexual stereotypes and distortions of the larger culture, reenactment of issues of power and domination related to gender will continue; sexual identity and sexual development will remain circumscribed by family silence and the sexist mandates of "normalcy" for women and men across the life span. Furthermore, sexual tension from any source in the family will be inadequately addressed without an analysis of power and gender dynamics.

Both Maddock (1990, 1997) and Schnarch (1991) recommended systemic approaches to clinical intervention with sexuality issues in the family. Maddock (1990) noted the importance of understanding value differences and the need for what he termed "a balanced interdependence of the genders as equally respected and valued modes of being-in-the-world . . . regardless of their perceived similarities and differences" (p. 59). His clinical recommendations for intervention focus on selecting broadly functional themes or issues for therapeutic intervention, negotiating priorities within the client ecosystem, and maintaining a dialectical balance of family interaction variables within the family system to facilitate transformation. However, family members have differing levels of power, influence, and resources, and any intervention will accordingly have a differing impact on each individual (Goldner, 1985). Leslie and Clossick (1992) stated explicitly: "Treating men and women as if they have the same options in relationships denies contextual realities. . . . Gender issues and their social context need to be talked about in therapy" (p. 258). The recommendations in Maddock's framework do not locate power and gender at the center of family transformation with sexuality issues.

The therapeutic framework for integrating sexual and marital therapy that was articulated by Schnarch (1991) promotes addressing physical contact and sexuality issues (even in the absence of identified sexual dysfunction) as a means of enhancing relatedness, bonding, and caregiving in the family unit. This framework, which Schnarch (1991) termed the "sexual crucible" (p. 19), focuses on a multidimensional clinical approach integrating systemic and object relations theories in the sexual arena, with an emphasis on developing the personal capacity for emotional intimacy and eroticism, which he defined as "the pursuit and delight in sensual pleasure" (p. 314). The psychological processes of the individual are related to the emotional legacies of the larger family system and thus contribute to the overall functioning of the sexual and marital relationship. According to Schnarch, it is the constructed social and personal context of the sexual relationship paradox (as represented by the unresolved problem or dilemma) that contains the blueprint for the developmental tasks that need to be accomplished.

This presentation of the interpersonal paradox that brings clients to counseling does not address the importance of understanding gendered experience. The description of incongruous power hierarchies in sexual relationships is grounded in the seeming contradictions of symptoms and control: The symptomatic partner, defined as the source of the problem or as less sexual, actually controls the sexual relationship. Although the role of culture in prescribing these incongruent sexual power hierarchies is addressed, it is only to note that current sex role stereotypes make dysfunction likely. No critical analysis of these stereotypes and their relationship to power and privilege is provided. Alternatively, the feminist perspective asserts that it is the rigid rules, expectations, and structures of patriarchal culture that create and maintain the paradox or dysfunction of the family system. As articulated by Goldner (1988), "As long as the world is an unfair place, as long as patriarchy prevails, love will be tainted by domination, subordination will be eroticized to make it tolerable, and symptoms will be necessary to keep families from flying apart" (p. 30).

The unit of analysis for Schnarch's (1991) framework, in the absence of power, gender, and racial considerations, remains the personal and interpersonal context, freed from the larger social context of inequalities that patriarchy structures into relationships (Hare-Mustin, 1998). The "sexual crucible" minimizes what Webster (1984) called "the vast organization of repression we confront as women" in developing an erotic self "with confidence and a realistic sense of self-preservation" (p. 396). How patriarchy and its effects on the family both maintain and perpetuate sexual oppression is unexamined. Feminist theory and analysis move beyond the limitations of this and other clinical frameworks that fail to address gender "as an indisputable category in exploring, understanding, and even changing, human experience and behavior" (Ellman & Taggert, 1998, p. 377).

Feminist Approaches to Sexual Issues in the Family

Dealing with sexuality in the family context presents opportunities for therapists and families to create a new vocabulary for a dialogue about sexual realities, drawing on the lived experiences of the men, women, adults, and children living in complex family configurations. Simply speaking about sexuality from a feminist perspective is a radical act. Naming and listening to narratives of lived experiences, and incorporating these realities into the relationship of feminist family therapy, create what Fine and Gordon (1992) recognized as the central dilemmas of praxis. That is, in the process of enacting a feminist agenda for prevention and intervention with families about sexuality, the contradictions, paradoxes, and hypocrisies embedded in the culture will emerge through all of the participants. Vigilance and the willingness to name and critique these elements as action and theory are merged are crucial components of transformation.

Feminist approaches to family therapy include a number of elements proposed from a variety of feminist perspectives (Worell & Remer, 1992). Some central goals have emerged in the discourse and development of feminist family therapy that have application to sexuality issues as well as other specific family life issues, and a number of these were articulated by Fish (1989). These include "a commitment to challenging the restrictions of traditional models of masculine and feminine socialization, bringing all family members to an awareness of the ways in which gender and sex role expectations are implicated in their problems, and assisting families to counteract the effects of sexism in their lives" (p. 311). The topic of sexuality and its expression in the family can serve to illuminate the lines of power, privilege, gender schemas, and limiting assumptions that may inhibit healthy sexual and interpersonal development within the family.

Counseling techniques for engaging the family and facilitating change are drawn from these goals. Creating a therapeutic environment focuses on demystifying the therapeutic process for the family. The work can be framed as collaborative and cooperative (Kogan, 1996). From another perspective, the therapist is viewed as more of a consultant than an expert, and encouragement is offered to enable all clients to value their own experiences and ways of making meaning of experience (Parvin & Biaggio, 1991). The emphasis on reducing the power differential between clients and therapists also may serve as a model for family and social relationships (Pilalis & Anderton, 1986). However, the implicitly hierarchical nature of the therapeutic relationship itself cannot be ignored, and the therapeutic relationship should be continuously examined to prevent replicating the dominant culture's power arrangements (Kogan, 1996). Counseling contracts are often developed "to articulate the conditions of therapy and the therapeutic goals toward which they will work" (Worell & Remer, 1992, p. 103).

Feminist family therapists also recognize that their own beliefs and values are present in their relationship with the family. Openness about these beliefs and philosophies is ethically necessary and creates the possibility of opening up dialogues within the family about topics that may have been ignored or suppressed. Unnoticed or invisible social sanctions can inhibit discussion and restrain meaning making on complex topics such as sexuality, sexual orientation, gender, and race (Kogan, 1996). By articulating a belief that sexuality is central to family life, a feminist family therapist can initiate the first step toward integrating a healthy approach to sexuality into the therapeutic process.

Questions about family life are a part of initial and subsequent family counseling sessions. Family therapists routinely ask questions about various aspects of family life that may not appear specifically related to the problem behavior (or behaviors) that stimulated the decision to seek help. Circular questioning about decision-making processes in the family, rules, family rituals, and the different activities of the family and its members gives information about family patterns of interaction, family values, and family relationships. From a feminist point of view, circular questioning about the specific problem illustrates the emotional and behavioral connections among and between family members related to the symptom and can lower intensity by leading the family to a more systemic perspective without sacrificing additional contextual information (Webb-Watson, 1987).

Specific questions about sex should be included that facilitate both sex role and power analyses. According to Worell and Remer (1992), such analyses increase the family's awareness of how sex role socialization has adversely affected them individually and as a family and how power differential according to gender is made explicit in the larger culture and the family. In initiating the conversation, the easier questions to ask first are about sexual values (Hof & Berman, 1986). Questions that could be asked include the following:

1. How did you (mother, father, stepparent, grandmother, or other adults in the family) learn about sex?
2. What were you taught about sexuality as a child?
3. What do you wish could have been different about your sex education?
4. Is sexuality a topic of conversation in your family? For everyone?
5. Who is responsible for talking with the children about sexuality?
6. How do you decide who talks with whom about sexuality?
7. When is it important for children to learn about sexuality?
8. What specifically do children need to know?
9. Do boys and girls get the same information in the family?
10. How has (will) the sexual curiosity of children been (be) handled in your family?
11. What does being male and being female mean to each of you in your family?
12. What are the rules about sexual behavior for each family member?

Reframing behavior through an analysis of sex roles and power changes the frame of reference for evaluating individual behavior, shifting the definition of problem issues from an intrapersonal–individual level to a societal–political level. From this perspective, family issues can be reframed as a social and cultural conflict, in which differing male–female socialization processes result in insufficient differentiation of identity and roles for family members, and thus contribute to family dysfunction. Relabeling behavior from this new perspective can change the label assigned to behavior from a negative connotation to a more adaptive or positive evaluation. The confusion and depression that followed the first sexual relationship of an adolescent girl with a boy from another race, and the subsequent family dissension, for example, take on new and expanded meaning when her family's beliefs about female sexuality, culture, and race are explored. Whereas heterosexual exploration may be encouraged or condoned in boys, such behavior is often pathologized or condemned in girls. Girls receive conflicting messages, such as that girls should be desirable but passive, sexual assertiveness is unattractive and dangerous, sexual availability is necessary to keep a boy interested, and girls are responsible for controlling sexual activity in a relationship and are responsible for sexual violence if it occurs (Ellman & Taggert, 1998; Fine, 1992; Hare-Mustin, 1998). Family and cultural beliefs about race and intimate relationships may be expressed only covertly but may be powerfully enforced. Understanding the family culture about sex, gender, and race is necessary to create a context for understanding behavior and linking it to the larger culture.

Opening this conversation about sex provides modeling opportunities for parents who wish to communicate more effectively with their children but feel incompetent or uncomfortable. Openness in communicating about sex is related more to a willingness to discuss particular issues than to self-disclosure regarding sexual behavior or practices (Walters & Walters, 1983). Often, there is a significant difference in the messages sent and received about sex. Through a therapist-initiated conversation on sexuality, the family can begin to reflect on its own experience, explore the meaning of sexual information as expressed in the family, and identify elements of family interaction for change.

Feminist family therapists facilitate the inclusion of women's and children's experience in the discussion and provide a focus on the way in which gender and power issues influence communication, choices, and attitudes about sexuality. For example, the adolescent girl dating the young man from a different race would be encouraged and supported in telling her own story about her relationship. She might be asked to describe and analyze her feelings about her choice of partner, her understanding of the sexual and racial taboos she violated, and the meaning of the experience to her. Leaving room for alternative explanations for behavior, and for the possibility of nontraditional choices and sexual orientations as potentially empowering and courageous, provides recognition of the many avenues for adolescents' self-expression and identity development (Tolman, 1994). These issues are particularly salient for gay and lesbian youths, who experience stigmatization and rejection from peers and families and are at greater risk for suicide (Erwin, 1993). Heterosexual presumption in the therapeutic discussion of sexual issues further alienates these teenagers and young adults and contributes to social isolation and the internalization of negative stereotypes.

Teaching relevant skills to family members helps them develop a larger array of coping strategies (Worell & Remer, 1992). Self-awareness and self-monitoring skills assist individuals in the family context to evaluate their own progress toward goals and their contributions to family efforts. Women especially need to develop the ability to identify and express needs and wants in the context of their role in the family, without subordination to the needs of others (Tolman, 1991, 1994). Teaching both individual and collaborative problem-solving skills that contradict the sex role stereotypes of behavior in the family can reduce the power differential across gender, facilitate reflection on sexual issues, and diminish conflict.

Developmental changes throughout the life span have implications for individual sexuality and for family interaction. Physiological changes, including those associated with puberty as well as later life, such as menopause and aging, alter personal and intrafamily dynamics through the meaning making associated with these changes. Discussing developmental changes provides a forum through which the family can adapt to the new circumstances and transform its meaning system to adjust to fundamental shifts in the family life cycle. Young children who explore their bodies and act on sexual curiosity may create anxiety in a family that is unprepared for overt sexual behavior. As adolescents begin romantic relationships, attitudes about sexuality may emerge that were never previously revealed in the family. Dealing with menstruation, contraception, and physical changes, including those related to sexual dysfunction, can alter family relationships. Other events may also affect family functioning, such as pregnancy and childbirth, divorce and remarriage of parents, and the partnering or marriage of older children. These changes are simultaneously sexual events and life cycle transitions, and they afford the family with the opportunity to renegotiate roles and expectations within the family, to adapt to and include new members, and to reevaluate values and beliefs regarding sexuality, intimacy, and sex roles (Maddock, 1983).

A straightforward approach to sexuality in the family also may enable the therapist to identify and address family secrets. The absence of discourse on gender and sex role issues restrains communication about important aspects of family life, including sexual abuse and domestic violence. The therapist should be prepared to address these potential issues if they emerge, drawing on feminist analyses to direct further intervention (Hare-Mustin, 1998; MacKinnon & Miller, 1985).

Case Study

Karen, 13 years old, is failing seventh grade and appears alternately depressed and angry in school, according to her teachers and the assistant principal, who referred her to a school-based family counselor. She has run away from home twice, returning 2 or 3 days later on her own. She reports being romantically involved with a boyfriend but has not revealed his name or the extent of their sexual relationship. She attends counseling with her parents, Anne and Bruce, and her 10-year-old sister, Kathryn. She has little to say during sessions and instead drapes herself in the chair looking tired and sometimes bored.

Anne appears angry and frustrated with her inability to influence her older daughter's behavior through either discussion or punishment. According to Anne, Karen's behavior began to change with her entry into middle school, marked by an increased interest in boys. In elementary school, Karen was reported to be an engaging and pleasant student who was active in soccer and a school chorus; her grades were excellent. She had a positive relationship with her sister and her father. Although Karen and her mother argued about Karen's lack of consistency in assuming household chores, Karen acknowledged that her relationship with both her parents had been close until recently.

Anne and Bruce never married, although they lived together for over 12 years in what both called a committed relationship. The couple ended their relationship when their younger daughter was 2 years old, after Bruce became involved with a woman who was a colleague in his work setting and later moved out. Anne then dated infrequently and did have one intimate relationship with a man for several months. Six years later, Bruce and Anne reconciled, and for nearly 2 years now, their relationship has continued, although Bruce has not moved back into the household at Anne's request. Throughout this entire period, Bruce remained an active parent to Karen and Kathryn, involved on a daily basis with transportation and regular visits, though the girls' primary residence continued to be with Anne. Both Anne and Bruce agree that their separation and subsequent reconciliation have been difficult for their daughters. Both girls pressed their parents to marry, but Anne insisted on a slow process of building a new relationship with Bruce.

In this session, Karen rolls her eyes when her mother points out the consequences of running away as including a "bad reputation." When the counselor asks Karen what her action indicated, she first says "nothing" but then adds that "my reputation has always been bad." When prompted further by the counselor to explain what a "bad reputation" means to her, Karen explains that because her parents never married, other people have regarded her family as permissive and "loose." According to Karen, her parents, and consequently herself, are seen as sexually promiscuous. Bruce and Anne appear shocked to hear these feelings. They report they all know other families with parents or partners who are not married and felt it was no longer such a moral issue. The counselor then prompts a discussion among all family members regarding their sexual values and beliefs for adults and children, as well as a clarification of Bruce and Anne's choices about marriage. By including circular questions about social expectations and sex role stereotypes, the counselor assists the family in exploring the implications of nontraditional choices for all family members and the different implications of a bad reputation for women and men.

Karen's behavior is explored further in the context of her perceived understanding of her family's belief system and her own developing sexuality. By defying cultural conventions, Karen may be attempting to establish a sense of self, an identity that acknowledges her own thoughts, feelings, and desires, although she is simultaneously at risk of losing relationships with others. Her family system is complex, and she receives conflicting messages from her parents in terms of their expectations of her behavior and their own actions. Although the systemic issues related to the family disruption and current status are also salient to Karen's difficulties, addressing sexual values, beliefs, and behaviors is considered central to enhancing understanding and open communication. During this developmental period in this family, both parents and children are coping with sexual identity and sexual transitions.

The feminist counselor in this case was sensitive to the sexual issues in the family, which enabled her to identify and comment on the implications of adult choices on the entire family. Furthermore, the counselor empowered the family to address this issue within the larger social context, in which nontraditional family configurations that contradict dominant cultural views on sexual relationships are viewed as problematic or immoral. By commenting on these sexual areas, the counselor brings the discourse of sexuality into the open and addresses the dilemmas of sexual desire, sexual identity, and family transition that make Karen vulnerable to harm: pregnancy, sexually transmitted diseases, getting a bad reputation, and school failure. Such a discussion also enables the family to challenge the limitations of cultural scripts that prohibit authentic and meaningful dialogue about sexuality with children and adolescents. The counselor thus invites the family members to explore their sexual ideologies and to construct a contextually meaningful response to Karen's situation.

Conclusion

Incorporating a feminist perspective on sexuality into family therapy has the potential to transform the family culture regarding sexuality. Gender oppression, heterosexual presumption, racism, and sex role stereotyping limit women and men in their ability to create and maintain healthy, intimate, and egalitarian relationships. Without intervention, families may perpetuate oppressive patterns related to sex education and sexual identity development. Feminist goals for therapy provide a template for engaging the family in a therapeutic conversation about sexuality, in contrast to the cultural taboo enforcing sexual silence beyond sex talk as a commodity in the social and economic marketplace.

This chapter attempts to begin the conversation about family sexuality from a feminist perspective and to offer some strategies for implementation in clinical practice. Promoting healthy family sexuality will necessitate education, training, and self-awareness about sex across gender, race, and culture on the part of the therapist. Self-awareness and a commitment to explore the ways in which the therapists' gender and their racial and sexual identity impact clinical work are imperative. Further research on sexuality using a feminist analysis is needed to provide more comprehensive and contextually authentic descriptions of women's and men's experiences from which theory and ethical practices can be developed.

References

Almeida, R., Woods, R., Messineo, T., & Font, R. (1998). The cultural context model: An overview. In F. Walsh (Ed.), *Normal family processes* (4th ed., pp. 414–432). New York: Guilford Press.

Almeida, R., Woods, R., Messineo, T., Font, R. J., & Heer, C. (1994). Violence in the lives of the racially and sexually different: A public and private dilemma. In R. Almeida (Ed.), *Expansions of feminist family therapy through diversity* (pp. 99–126). New York: Harrington Park Press.

Avis, J. M. (1988). Deepening awareness: A private study guide to feminism and family therapy. *Journal of Psychotherapy and the Family, 3,* 15–46.

Barnett, J. K., Papini, D. R., & Gbur, E. (1991). Familial correlates of sexually active pregnant and nonpregnant adolescents. *Adolescence, 26*, 457–472.

Benshoff, J. M., & Alexander, S. J. (1993). The family communication project: Fostering parent–child communication about sexuality. *Elementary School Guidance, 27*, 288–300.

Calderone, M. (1984). Above and beyond politics: The sexual socialization of children. In C. Vance (Ed.), *Pleasure and danger: Exploring female sexuality* (pp. 131–136). Boston: Routledge & Kegan Paul.

Christensen, C. P. (1988). Issues in sex therapy with ethnic and minority women. *Women and Therapy, 7*, 187–206.

Echols, A. (1984). The taming of the id. In C. Vance (Ed.), *Pleasure and danger: Exploring female sexuality* (pp. 50–72). Boston: Routledge & Kegan Paul.

Ellman, B., & Taggert, M. (1998). Changing gender norms. In F. Walsh (Ed.), *Normal family processes* (4th ed., pp. 377–404). New York: Guilford Press.

Erwin, K. (1993). Interpreting the evidence: Competing paradigms and the emergence of lesbian and gay suicide as a "social fact." *International Journal of Health Services, 23*, 437–453.

Fine, M. (Ed.). (1992). *Disruptive voices: The possibilities of feminist research*. Ann Arbor: University of Michigan Press.

Fine, M., & Gordon, S. (1992). Feminist transformations of/despite psychology. In M. Fine (Ed.), *Disruptive voices: The possibilities of feminist research* (pp. 1–27). Ann Arbor: University of Michigan Press.

Fine, M., & Macpherson P. (1992). Over dinner: Feminism and adolescent female bodies. In M. Fine (Ed.), *Disruptive voices: The possibilities of feminist research* (pp. 175–204). Ann Arbor: University of Michigan Press.

Fish, L. S. (1989). Comparing structural, strategic, and feminist-informed family therapies: Two Delphi studies. *American Journal of Family Therapy, 17*, 303–314.

Goldner, V. (1985). Warning: Family therapy may be hazardous to your health. *Family Networker, 9*, 19–23.

Goldner, V. (1988). Generation and gender: Normative and covert hierarchies. *Family Process, 27*, 17–31.

Gray, L. A., House, R. M., & Eicken, S. (1996). Human sexuality instruction for couple and family counselor educators. *Family Journal, 4*, 208–216.

Hare-Mustin, R. T. (1998). Challenging traditional discourses in psychotherapy: Creating space for alternatives. *Journal of Feminist Family Therapy, 10*(3), 39–56.

Hof, L., & Berman, E. (1986). The sexual genogram. *Journal of Marital and Family Therapy, 12*(1), 39–47.

Johnson, T. W., & Keren, M. S. (1998). The families of lesbian women and gay men. In M. McGoldrick (Ed.), *Re-visioning family therapy: Race, culture, and gender in clinical practice* (pp. 320–329). New York: Guilford Press.

Kogan, S. (1996). Clinical praxis: Examining culture and power in family therapy. *Journal of Feminist Family Therapy, 8*(3), 25–44.

Leslie, L., & Clossick, M. L. (1992). Changing set: Teaching family therapy from a feminist perspective. *Family Relations, 41*, 256–263.

Lerner, H. G. (1987). Is family systems theory really systemic? A feminist communication. *Journal of Psychotherapy and the Family, 3*, 47–63.

MacKinnon, L., & Miller, D. (1985). The sexual component in family therapy: A feminist critique. *Journal of Social Work and Human Sexuality, 3*, 81–101.

Maddock, J. (1983). Human sexuality in the lifecycle of the family system. In R. Woody & J. Woody (Eds.), *Sexual issues in family therapy* (pp. 1–31). Rockville, MD: Aspen.

Maddock, J. W. (1990). Promoting healthy family sexuality. *Journal of Family Psychotherapy, 1*(1), 49–63.

Maddock, J. W. (1997). Sexuality education: A history lesson. *Journal of Psychology and Human Sexuality, 9*(3–4), 1–22.

Nichols, M. P., & Schwartz, R. C. (1998). *Family therapy: Concepts and methods* (4th ed.) Needham Heights, MA: Allyn & Bacon.

Parvin, R., & Biaggio, M. K. (1991). Paradoxes in the practice of family therapy. *Women and Therapy, 11*(2), 3–12.

Pilalis, J., & Anderton, J. (1986). Feminism and family therapy: A possible meeting point. *Journal of Family Therapy, 8*, 99–114.

Ross, E., & Rapp, R. (1983). Sex in society: A research note from social history and anthropology. *Comparative Studies in Society and History, 23*, 51–72.

Rubin, G. (1984). Thinking sex: Notes for a radical theory of the politics of sexuality. In C. Vance (Ed.), *Pleasure and danger: Exploring female sexuality* (pp. 267–319). Boston: Routledge & Kegan Paul.

Santelli, J. S., & Beilenson, P. (1992). Risk factors for adolescent sexual behavior, fertility and sexually transmitted diseases. *Journal of School Health, 62*, 271–279.

Schnarch, D. (1991). *Constructing the sexual crucible: An integration of sexual and marital therapies.* New York: Norton.

Tiefer, L. (1996a). The medicalization of sexuality: Conceptual, normative, and professional issues. *Annual Review of Sex Research, 7*, 252–282.

Tiefer, L. (1996b). Towards a feminist sex therapy. *Women and Therapy, 19*(4), 53–64.

Tolman, D. H. (1991). Adolescent girls, women and sexuality: Discerning dilemmas of desire. *Women and Therapy, 11*(4), 55–69.

Tolman, D. H. (1994). Doing desire: Adolescent girls' struggles for/with desire. *Gender and Society, 8*, 324–342.

Vance, C. (1984). Pleasure and danger: Towards a politics of sexuality. In C. Vance (Ed.), *Pleasure and danger: Exploring female sexuality* (pp. 1–30). Boston: Routledge & Kegan Paul.

Vance, C., & Pollis, C. (1990). Introduction: A special issue on feminist perspectives on sexuality. *Journal of Sex Research, 27*, 1–5.

Walters, J., & Walters, L. H. (1983). The role of the family in sex education. *Journal of Research and Development in Education, 16*(2), 8–15.

Webb-Watson, L. (1987). Women, family therapy, and the larger systems. *Journal of Psychotherapy and the Family, 3,* 145–156.

Webster, P. (1984). The forbidden: Eroticism and taboo. In C. Vance (Ed.), *Pleasure and danger: Exploring female sexuality* (pp. 385–398). Boston: Routledge & Kegan Paul.

Worell, J., & Remer, P. (1992). *Feminist perspectives in therapy: An empowerment model for women.* West Sussex, England: Wiley.

Yarber, W. L., & Parrillo, A. V. (1992). Adolescents and sexually transmitted diseases. *Journal of School Health, 62,* 331–350.

■ ■ ■

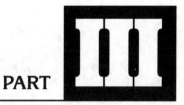

PART

AN INTERVIEW WITH
A LEADING FEMINIST
FAMILY THERAPIST

10

An Interview With
Cheryl Rampage

Cheryl Rampage, PhD
Kathleen M. May, PhD

KM: How did you become involved in feminist family therapy?

CR: Like many people in the sixties and seventies, I lived my life in a couple of different tracks. I started graduate school in '73, by which time I was already a feminist. When I got to graduate school, I knew I wanted to study clinical psychology. The first

Cheryl Rampage, PhD, is one of the leading authorities on feminist family therapy. Her coauthored book *Feminist Family Therapy: A Casebook* (Goodrich, Rampage, Ellman, & Halstead, 1988) is considered a classic in the field. She is currently on the faculty of The Family Institute at Northwestern University. The institute is the Midwest's oldest and largest center providing counseling services, training, and research in couples and family therapy.

Dr. Rampage received her doctorate from Loyola University of Chicago. She is an approved supervisor by the American Association for Marriage and Family Therapy and has been involved in training and supervision of family therapists for approximately 20 years. She also maintains her own clinical caseload. Dr. Rampage has written numerous articles and book chapters on feminist couples and family therapy as well as feminist training and supervision. She lives in the Chicago area with her husband and their son and daughter. This interview took place at The Family Institute in the winter of 1999.

semester that I was in graduate school, I was taking abnormal psychology, and I decided to try to write something about women and psychotherapy. But what I found was that there were very, very few resources. I think I came across Phyllis Chesler's book *Women and Madness* (Chesler, 1972), which had recently been published. When I looked at the psychotherapy literature, most of it was extremely sexist. The few things I found about women's psychotherapy were about how crazy we were. I wrote a paper based on the few resources that I could find, and my professor really ripped it apart. After that, I just kind of put that aside for a while.

KM: A male professor?

CR: Yes—a male professor. He thought there weren't very many citations, and there wasn't much methodology behind working with women, it was like working with men, and what's this all about anyway? He thought I should have chosen a better topic. Then I actually started doing clinical work. As I did clinical work, it became apparent to me, particularly when I worked with couples, that issues around gender, sexism, and patriarchy were just all over the place. But I had no way in which to speak about it. So I was a good girl, a good student, read all the books, did the work, and got the degree. Then, lo and behold, right after I got my degree in 1978, Rachel Hare-Mustin published a paper called "A Feminist Approach to Family Therapy." It was such a defining moment. I felt like, "Oh, my God. So, here's a grown-up, I had heard of her, and knew that she was a famous person. If she could say these things, all of which made perfect sense to me, then maybe it could actually come into the therapy room."

By that time, I was on the faculty of The University of Houston at Clear Lake, teaching in family therapy, and it was only a year after my degree so I decided to get some postdegree training. The Galveston Family Institute was being formed at that time. I started in this commuter program, one Saturday a month or something. It was a very small group, four people, and this one person from Houston named Thelma Jean Goodrich. She's over at Baylor, and she is a feminist. Galveston is 50 miles from Houston, where I also lived, so we decided to carpool. Every Saturday we would drive back and forth on the Gulf freeway, and there's nothing to look at on the Gulf freeway (laughter); there's nothing to do but talk. We started talking about how what we were learning, mostly behind the one-way mirror as we were trained back then, was just rubbing us the wrong way in certain areas. And the areas were usually about power and gender.

At the end of that year, a couple of other friends of ours were in another training program at Galveston Family Institute, and we formed a study group. We started reading various books and journals, including Rachel Hare-Mustin's (1978, 1987) work. The Stone Center was starting to publish, and we read *In a Different Voice* (Gilligan, 1982). You know that Paul Simon song, "Why don't we get together and call ourselves an Institute?" That's what we did.

We started with a workshop on feminist therapy. A small group, almost all women, attended. There were a couple of men there, both of whom asked questions immediately. They were both angry and felt that we had been disrespectful to them or we were making a problem where one didn't exist. Afterwards, women came up to us and said, "Thank God you are talking about this stuff" and "Please do it some more." That emboldened us enough to form The Women's Institute for Life Studies. We started off offering a few workshops and a monthly salon where we'd invite people to come in and talk about topics of the day within family therapy. That was how it began.

KM: Will you talk a little about *Feminist Family Therapy: A Casebook* (Goodrich, Rampage, Ellman, & Halstead, 1988)?

CR: We had submitted a proposal on gender and marital therapy for the 1984 American Association for Marital and Family Therapy's conference, which was noted by an editor with Norton who was looking for new books to publish. She invited us to dinner, and we thought, "Oh, this will be cool; let's go to San Francisco and have dinner with the editor. Oh my God, this is so exciting." So we did—thinking we were kids playing make believe. Then we met the editor, Susan, and she was having none of it. She was just like totally grown up, and she said, "There's not a book in the field on gender and therapy, which is going to be a hot topic. Make a proposal." So we went back to Houston, and Thelma Jean said, "OK, let's do this." She really had us going, and that is how she became first author of the book. The journey was really about trying to figure out how all the political stuff that I was learning in the world could come into my work as a clinician. And it really was only when I was in the company of like-minded women over an extended period of time that I was able to get myself to think clearly and hold onto my thoughts well enough to start formulating a real critique.

KM: Whom would you consider your influences?

CR: The first time I actually met Rachel Hare-Mustin (laughing), I
went up to her and said, "I'm so glad to meet you; you're my
ego ideal." And she said, "I've never been anybody's ego ideal"
(laughter), so I'd have to say Rachel. Rachel has always been
tremendously generous about reading work, critiquing it, and
making referrals for writing and speaking opportunities. She's
been wonderful. Also the Women's Project[1] people, Olga
Silverstein, Betty Carter, Marianne Walters, and Peggy Papp,
were instrumental in our work. After we did our presentation
at the Stone Center,[2] Betty Carter wrote us a letter. It was only
a sentence or two, but we considered it fan mail, and we were
very excited. We pasted it up on the wall in the office for months.
It was so gratifying. Monica McGoldrick was also very helpful
to us. I think all of those people influenced me a great deal.
One of the very encouraging things that happened at the Stone
Center conference was that the Women's Project people shared
their experiences about writing their book. We were in the midst
of writing our book at that point, so it was particularly meaningful. We were quite far into it and struggling with it. They
told these wonderful stories about experiences that were similar
to our experiences. For instance, they were not all in the same
city, so they would agree to get together for a weekend. The
first thing they would do is go shopping, then they would eat,
then they would pass around work. Each of them would read
the other's work, and they would offer some critique. Then
they would cry because everybody would be hurt 'cause the
other person didn't like their work. This is stuff that we were
all experiencing constantly.
Each of us would write a piece and then come back together
and talk about it. We had made a commitment not to send
anything off that we didn't all agree on. So that meant we had

---

[1]Marianne Walters, Betty Carter, Peggy Papp, and Olga Silverstein created
The Women's Project in Family Therapy in 1977. They were committed to
exploring the concerns and experiences of women in families and to bringing
feminist consciousness into the mainstream of family therapy. They offered
workshops around the United States, and in 1988 they published their book
The Invisible Web: Gender Patterns in Family Relationships.
[2]Dr. Rampage presented a paper with the other authors of the book *Feminist Family Therapy: A Casebook* on working with lesbian couples in family
therapy in September 1986 at the second conference of The Stone Center for
Developmental Services and Studies, Wellesley, Massachusetts.

to negotiate a lot. We found it hard that somebody would write something and someone else would say, "Well, you know, I just don't think that it's really quite like that." And the person might begin to cry and feel hurt. There was stuff that just had to be on a process level, which had to get worked through. That often doesn't happen. First of all, there are not that many joint-authored books—for that reason, it is hard. Second, when there are such books, it's usually, "You write chapter one, you write chapter two, you write chapter three." We were writing every chapter together and consulting on all these cases. It was a very intense kind of process that ultimately was very rewarding, but very challenging. Hearing the Women's Project people talk about their own process was very affirming. We could get through this too, with our struggles and fears, and whatever. Our process was no crazier than theirs was, and so it was OK.

KM: Do you consider yourself a maverick?

CR: A maverick? Well, I was really raised as a good Catholic girl. So I have a very conventional approach to life fundamentally. But for some reason, and I think it's got to do with the fact that I am pretty smart and I wasn't very cute as an adolescent, so getting all mixed up with boys wasn't an issue. I stayed smart and interested in intellectual matters. And I was growing up in a time when issues of justice and fairness were coming to the forefront because of the civil rights movement. I got very fired up about that. And so even though I come from a very conservative family, in my own way of living conservative, I became very infused with concerns and passions around justice and fairness. I think that was the basis of my interest in feminism. I certainly have nothing against men as people, but I have a lot against patriarchy as a system, and I think that marriage is a patriarchal institution. Every marriage is drenched in issues around gender. It seemed to me that it wasn't a radical act—it was a self-preserving act.

If I hadn't become a feminist, I would have thought I was crazy. If you are not a feminist, there's no other way to explain some of the things that happen in the world that create such disadvantage for the female, except that there must be something wrong with her. So I've always said, "The only safe female is a feminist because even if it doesn't stop you from being raped, abused, beaten, or whatever, at least you know something about what it is about. You have a way of thinking about it that doesn't make it about you."

I suppose I am a maverick in the ways I've thought about bringing gender into therapy. Certainly, I haven't been extreme, but then I've been received often as this kind of fringe, maverick person. I've had men in the field who've met me and said, "Oh, you're nothing like what I thought." And I've said, "Well, what were you thinking?" They said, "I just thought you'd be taller." (Laughter) People have actually said that. "And I thought you'd be much angrier." Now I'm not exactly sure where that comes from, 'cause my reading of my writing is not that it's angry, it is that it is firm, and it speaks to what I think is true and in an unwavering way. I don't feel like I've got these axes to grind. I've been deeply in love with my husband for 20 something years. I adore my son, and I adore my daughter as well. If I've any axes to grind, it's not at people, it's the system that I've always felt was unfair, especially when I think of my grandmother's time.

KM: I know you dedicated your first book to your mothers. I loved the quote "because they gave us the ability to question" (Goodrich et al., 1988).

CR: Right, we thought a long time about how to dedicate the book, and we decided that we would like to dedicate it to our mothers. We wanted it to be an honest dedication. We didn't want it to be, "Oh, our mothers are so wonderful and strong and brave," because our mothers were all caught in all the conventional issues of being in a patriarchal society. Our mothers were all very loving, and we decided that we could say that because we felt so loved, it allowed us to be in places where we felt solid enough that we were able to question. That is how we decided to dedicate the book. I think we all remain fond of the dedication.

KM: Is your husband a feminist?

CR: Yes, my husband is definitely a feminist; not a self-identified feminist but he is a feminist. And my children are likewise. One of the most successful days I had, as a mother, was the day my daughter was talking to me about some boy who had made a sexist comment. My daughter, who was in fourth grade at the time, said, "And I said to him, 'Excuse me, you cannot say something like that just because I'm a girl.'" And I said, "Oh really?" And she said, "Well, of course, I'm a feminist; I wouldn't put up with that." And I said, "You are!" (Laughter) And she looked at me and she said, "What do you think?" It was nice to know that I had not yet started proselytizing her, but she had taken up the cause.

KM: Some of my graduate students have a very difficult time with the label "feminist." They do seem to be for the equality of women, aware of gender stereotypes and power issues, but they do not accept the label.

CR: I think that's very common. Most women nowadays by 30 or so are taking positions, having beliefs about themselves that are entirely feminist, but they reject the label. That's all they are rejecting. Why do they reject the label? I think they reject the label because they see it as unfeminine, which is really a shame. I'm afraid that it still puts them at risk not to label themselves as feminists. Without that framework, it can get really cloudy. You can think that you have this good job, and you have a husband who does the dishes, because you're just such a strong, good person rather than because, for 25 years now, your mother and your sisters have been hammering away at this issue.

Every time I hear the phrase "postfeminist," the skin on the back of my neck crawls. A recent example of that was when I was with my husband at this wonderful resort in California. He was working, and I was just hanging around the pool, feeling like I was in the lap of luxury. So I'm sitting there on a Sunday afternoon thinking, "Oh, I'll just read the *New York Times*," my favorite thing to do on a Sunday. In the magazine, there is an article about what the sex experts have to say in the Clinton/Lewinsky era. Of course, I read it. It's full of stuff that I think is just garbage. One of the sex experts was saying, "Well, what this proves is that monogamy is just too constraining. People can't do monogamy." But the one that really got to me was the one that said, "The problem with the whole thing was that Clinton didn't realize that Monica Lewinsky was a postfeminist woman. She's used to using her sexuality to do what she wants and is not constrained by old ideas about sexuality." Something like that. I just about blew a gasket. I was so upset, I had to get a legal pad, write a letter to the editor, and then chase down the business office at the Ritz-Carlton to make them type up my letter.

What I basically said was, "Look, if what postfeminism means is that women are now freer, less inhibited about satisfying male sexual appetite, then we need to take a step back and look back at feminism, which was about reciprocity, mutuality, and respect. If Monica Lewinsky was in a position to understand that she should be able to receive as much as she gets in a sexual relationship, this whole thing never would have happened to begin with." That is my concern about this idea of postfeminism. First of all, I think it is a way to try and get rid of feminism: Okay we did that, it is over with, we don't need it anymore because we solved those problems. Second, it allows women, particularly, as you were mentioning your concern about younger women, to delude themselves that all they need to do is be strong and everything will equalize out, that they won't have to face any of the issues that are still on the table.

Almost all the issues are still on the table, although none of them are in the same place they were 25 years ago. Women have not reached equity in pay. They are still victimized in the divorce courts. Twenty-two percent of American women feel that their husbands have forced sex on them, while only 3% of the husbands feel that they have ever forced sex. What is this about? That's a big gender difference, and it has to do with mutuality, consent, and reciprocity. Those issues are still out there, and if we don't have a feminist perspective on them, then we are at risk of thinking whatever goes wrong, it must be us.

KM: What do you think of "gender-sensitive therapy"? Is it an embracement of feminist family therapy or is it in total opposition?

CR: I don't think it's in total opposition. I think it's been watered down from feminist family therapy. It's an attempt to say that gender matters, we have to understand it, but we don't want to be political about it. I think we cannot not be political about gender. Gender is political. I prefer the label of feminist. I'm very clear what I talk about, what I write about, and what it means. It is not man hating; it's not female supremacy; it's not the death of the family; it's just about equality and opportunity. That is what it is about.

I think when people write about gender-sensitive therapy, what they are saying is, "I'm not really comfortable with the feminist stuff or I think it will devalue me to label myself that way. I know it's something about gender, but I'm not going to put it into a political context. Therefore, all I'm saying is, men and women seem to be different, and women complain that they don't feel as equal." They usually aren't including any kind of political analysis of power, and I think that that's an absolutely essential piece of doing feminist therapy. Feminist therapy is about analyzing and unpacking assumptions and manifestations of power, particularly in couple relationships but also in all other kinds of relationships.

KM: Any thoughts on social constructivism?

CR: I mostly think of myself as a social constructionist. I told you before that I'm really a good girl, so there are some things that I think are almost innate. I don't know where they come from, but they seem to be there from the git-go (laughing), and they are there no matter what I do. I do think that a lot of how we experience the world, we experience because of how we define the meaning of it, and that is a kind of social constructionism. So, I do believe that people have some choice, and I can help them facilitate that choice to construct their modes of living differently in ways that might make life easier or more satisfying to them. Likewise, I think that gender is a social construction. Saying that doesn't mean that if you decide you don't like the social construction, you could just change it. Some social constructions are held in place by things that are larger than personal preferences. They are held in place by whole systems of rules, customs, rituals, and history that support a particular kind of social construction.

I was talking with my kids the other day about how research has shown, that from the first minute of life, people feel compelled to genderize babies—the pink and blue blankets. They give them all these attributions: Little boys are tougher, little girls are prettier, and on and on. My daughter said, "Well, they could just put them all in white blankets." And I said, "OK, let's picture the nursery all in white blankets, and you don't know the gender of any of the babies in the nursery. What do you think that would be like?" And she said, "Well, I think people would just take the diapers off and see. They would want to know." So we started talking a little bit about why that is.

Here's a social construction for you. People assume that once you know the sex or gender of somebody, you know all kinds of things about him or her. That's a social construction that I would very much like to see changed. But that particular social construction requires a paradigm shift on a large order, which I think we are in the midst of. It's such a huge paradigm shift and permeates every aspect of all of our lives. It's going to take generations to complete it. But I think it will happen. I think it's consistent with the global impulses and movements toward equality and democracy in the world. Gender will be the final struggle. There are many race struggles in the world, but they are not because most of us think we are the superior race. Most of the civilized world believes people ought not to be dealt with on the basis of their racial and cultural makeup.

We ought not to be prejudiced on that basis. Most of the civilized, educated part of our world believes conceptually that that's true. Of course, there's often a difference between our theories and our practices, and I think that's where the difficulty is now.

KM: Do you think our societal institutions have kept pace with the changes?

CR: I think women have driven the change, and they have had the greatest influence first on their immediate worlds—in their families. I certainly do think that they have had some impact on the political process and on the work world. I was talking with somebody the other day about what made the current women's movement possible. We talked about the movement as an offshoot of the civil rights movement and as an offshoot of a general movement toward protecting and respecting human rights around the world. But then she said, "You know, it really was possible because of birth control." And soon as she said that I thought, "You know, that is true."

Until women got control of their bodies and didn't have to worry about pregnancy every year and the possibility of an early death from the complications of pregnancies, how could they change the way they related to the world? They were bound to the world by their reproductive life. When that changed, it made possible other kinds of changes. There have been ups and downs along the way, but I think starting in the late 1960s and early 1970s, the movement toward thinking that women ought not to be deprived of opportunity in the world because of their gender has really taken hold in our society. I don't see us going back. I do see a backlash of various sorts, but I don't think the backlash is going to have any kind of serious detrimental impact. I think this is just too consistent with what I consider basic human impulses for decency and respect.

KM: It is my experience in the universities that any writings on women's issues or from a feminist perspective are still devalued, not considered scholarship per se. Do you see that?

CR: Oh, yes. I think most women experience that. I think it is slowly changing, but the reason why it is slow to change is because women are still primarily nurtured by men, because the higher up you go in the academy, the fewer women there are. Until a powerful woman says, "You write on that, that's fine. You can do really good work and can get recognition. I'm on this awards committee, and that's the kind of things we like to see." Women will continue to feel discouraged by very sexist mentors, who may think truly, "I'm doing you a favor here. Don't get yourself into this ghetto of talking about women's stuff. Do some real research; talk about something that's going to be fundable and cutting edge in your field." I don't think the purpose is to keep women down, although it's tremendously discouraging as a woman who has interests in women's issues to hear that. The effect overall is discouraging to women, and the solution is to have more women mentoring, more women on editorial boards and as ad hoc reviewers for journals, and as deans and provosts who make tenure decisions, and all that kind of stuff. In all of our society, the academy is one of slowest places to change. So, it's not surprising that it is somewhat demoralizing.

KM: Some people would say that women, particularly women who have made it, don't really seem to want to mentor women.

CR: Can we attack that for a minute? I think there are some things that are worth looking at. One thing is if we are talking about women who are over 50 or so who are now in a position to mentor, they were almost all mentored by men because that is who was there. Many women paid a huge price to get to where they are. There may be a certain number of individuals who seem to give off the aura that, "Look, I had to crawl my way up here; you've just got to do it. I am not going to give anyone else an easy hand; no one gave me an easy hand. I really had to work my butt off and be twice as good as everybody else to get where I am now." So there's that.

Another thing is that one of the dilemmas that successful women face is the requirements for being successful in the academy or in industry are usually somewhat different than the requirements to be a good mentor. And if you are a man and a mentor, then you are being generous and wonderful, and "look at how much you are giving." If you are a woman and mentor, it can be seen as "you're mothering." It can be devalued because it is the woman who's doing it.

I don't feel that I was ever mentored well in graduate school because my interests were not anything that anyone else was interested in. The mentoring that I had was after graduate school, and it was by the senior women in the field whom I was talking about earlier. There was a certain amount of raising each other up, kind of as siblings, that women in my cohort had done. My generation of women who came into the field in the late 1970s and early 1980s really nurtured each other. We were not mentored. We were not senior to each other, but we were all struggling with similar ideas and similar dilemmas, and we just tried to support each other and help to get a problem solved. That has probably been the most helpful input that I have had from anybody.

KM: And do you have that locally now?

CR: I have a little of it locally. What I would consider my closest intellectual colleagues are not local. They are a group of women whom I met because we all presented on the national circuit. And at some point, we decided, "Since what we really go to these conferences for is to see each other, why don't we just see each other, and skip the conferences." So there are six women, including myself, who meet once or twice a year for a long weekend. We consult with each other, spend time together, all kinds of things. We have been meeting for 3 or 4 years now and have become extremely close. We seem to have a ritual. We go through everyone's current vitamin and hormone regimen, and what we have read, fiction and nonfiction, in and out of the field, and how all our families are doing. Then during the weekend, each of us gets at least a 2-hour consultation from the rest of the group about what we are currently working on. We met a few weeks ago and I was getting ready to deliver a big paper, so I asked for a consultation on my paper. Someone else might be working out some issues that she wants to write about, or what she may be thinking about her relationship to money or whatever. It's a very inclusive kind of comprehensive consulting. Because we now have a history, people can say, "Remember last year when you were working on that piece, this sounds similar, but I think you're now in a place where you can really do something about it." It's really nice to have that kind of camaraderie. It's been fabulous.

KM: Are you pleased with clinical training today in terms of coverage of gender and power issues and . . .

CR: I don't think that the field quite knows how to deal with this. I don't hold family therapy, psychology, or any other field responsible. We know now that issues of difference, whether it's gender, culture, race, class, are significant issues, but we don't quite know what's the best way to bring those issues into training programs. It is still being done in fairly piecemeal fashion for the most part, as I understand it. We are trying to give people so much in such a limited period of time. Even at the master's level, and I suspect at the doctoral level, it is very difficult to weave in as much as you would like to, or weave it in the best way, whatever that is. I am not even sure how to deal with these issues. At some point we said, "Okay, we have to have a class, a class in race and culture, a class in gender." But then everybody says, "Okay, that is done, they did gender over there so, don't worry about that now, we will just do therapy." I don't think that's the best way to train.

It would be better if we could always be conscious about how these issues are affecting our work, whether therapy or teaching, whatever. I think that's been really difficult to manage. If you try to put it everywhere, you're always saying, "Oh yeah, remember race, class, gender?" And if you put it in one course, then it's ghettoized, and becomes marginalized. I don't think we are doing as well as we might. I'm not quite sure about the best way to do it.

I do like one of the things we've done here. In our experiential training model, we treat gender as a coequal level of a category of analysis with generation, with culture, with organization, with sequence. There are seven categories of analysis we call meta-frameworks. We try to teach the students always to think. "Okay, so you've got this system. What are the developmental issues? What are the gender issues? What are the social and cultural issues? What are the issues about family of origin? What are the issues about organization and structure?" We encourage students always to be at least flipping through these lenses.

Sometimes, for example, when I'm dealing with a family with an acting-out adolescent, the gender issue may not be so prominent. It's still there, but here's some kid who's threatening suicide or running away. The subtleties of the way gender is held in place within the marriage is not going to come to the forefront. So in that situation, you're looking at something else. Anytime you have a heterosexual couple, I don't know how you can not think of gender, because the extent to which any of us experiences our gender in the presence of the other gender is so enormous, especially if you are negotiating an intimate or close relationship. You just cannot not think about these things. They cannot not be influential, let me say that.

KM: My partner had a good laugh at me last night. I am not sure what I was thinking. I had been to a conference and rushed home to unpack and pack again and I said, "Do you think I could wear slacks?" And he asked, "Did you really say that?"

CR: (Laughter)

KM: I don't know how that could come out of my mouth, but it did.

CR: It's funny you said that. Last weekend at a conference, Terence Real, who wrote *I Don't Want to Talk About It* (Real, 1998) on

covert male depression was the primary speaker on Friday; I
was the primary speaker on Saturday. So I had the opportunity to hear him; he didn't hear me. On Saturday morning in
front of the audience, I said, "We are talking basically about
the same stuff, but I'm going to approach it in a different way.
Let me just highlight a couple of the differences that come to
my mind about how we think about this issue." And I said a
couple of things. Then, I said, "Third, I can pretty much guar-
antee you that I spent a lot more time thinking about what I
was going to wear today than he did." Then I went into this
little analysis, which was quite true, that he got up in the morning
and put on his black turtleneck, his black sport coat, his black
pants, you know, very New York, and comes here. Because
he's a guy and he is big, which is a good thing, he doesn't look
like a wimp at all. He is masculine looking in the traditional
sense of masculine. Nobody is going to think, "Oh, is he really
man enough." Me, I am a really small person, and I have to
worry about whether I am going to look big and strong enough
to be saying what I want to say, and have people really listen
to me. And at the same time, am I going to be feminine and
soft enough so they won't think, "Oh, my God, is this just another angry woman, one of those man-haters?" I am sitting there
trying to balance these competing demands, and by the way
my feet are 48 years old, I don't want to be too uncomfortable,
I've got this hip problem, and I'm still fighting with my body
image. So I've got all of these things that are controlling and
constraining me around what I wear that he didn't even have
to think about. He got to spend 25 more minutes thinking about
what he was going to say today than I did. The audience got a
laugh out of that. But of course, it was true! There is a perfect
example of a gender difference.
Now, there are some women who will get up and not even think
about what they are going to wear, but I'm not one of them. I
am trying to position myself in a very particular way with my
audience so that I cannot be dismissed, and that means for me
at my age, my culture, my class, I must look professional, I
must look feminine, and I must look strong. I have to look sober
and serious. You know, it takes a lot (laughter) to pull all that
together. It's just not that easy.

KM: It's funny too, because when I was preparing for this I thought,
"Okay, in 1988 Cheryl was already a tenured associate professor." Then I thought, "I wonder how old she is," and now I
realize I am only one year younger.

CR: There you go.

KM: But not quite as accomplished . . .

CR: One of the nice things that has happened to me as a developmental psychologist in the last 20 years is a kind of rewriting of life span development. That now includes the possibility, both to women and men, and I think it was women who thought this up, that our life spans are going to include many phases at various times and we will be differentially attached to families, to work, to leisure at different stages. It is not like, "All right, now you're in your 20s, so you must earn your degree, then you must work, and then you must do family stuff." It is going to work out differently for different people, with lots of variation. Within our generation, there are women who disrupted their professional lives, and sometimes their education, to take time out. For 10 or 15 years, they put their energy into their family lives. Then they come back to the workforce and have tremendous energy for their professional careers, only they are starting at a different age.

Almost all men take no time off. That often makes women feel like they are working so hard and will never catch up, which is too bad. Rachel [Hare-Mustin] was one of the people who first talked about this issue because she didn't get her degree until she was older and had raised kids She was in her 40s when she got her PhD. Many of the women I know who have been very productive in their careers got their degrees in their 50s and 60s. I know someone in her 80s still working, well, she is just retiring (laughter). There are certainly many different paths.

KM: We mentioned race and class earlier. A criticism that I've heard about feminist family therapists is that they represent only a small percentage of women, those who are White, at least middle class, educated, and heterosexual. I certainly found your book to be an exception to that, but do you think that criticism merits any consideration?

CR: The whole contemporary women's movement certainly started off as an upper-middle-class phenomenon. I don't think that's continued. I do think that the women's movement has embraced women of color, but the leadership in the women's movement started out in the White, educated, middle class. From what I hear from African American women, they always are aware of feeling some bind when gender is emphasized, because for them, when they think of oppression, they think of race. They don't want that to be misconstrued because race is so prominent, it is so defining for them. Then second, they have this complication. They know that African American men are the most oppressed people by White society. They feel very reluctant to challenge those men or attack those who are sexist as a feminist because they do not want to side with the White oppressive elements of our society. I think it's a complicated bind. I've never had a conversation with an African American woman who didn't know or couldn't articulate that there were issues about being a woman that were separate from issues about being an African American that informed who she was, and what her experiences were.

I also think that in terms of sexual orientation, the feminist movement has actually been very inclusive of lesbian women. Perhaps not as much as one would like, but certainly lesbians were much embraced compared with our society in general where heterosexuality and being male were all powerful. The women's movement was much more tolerant and accepting, at some costs, because they had to take a lot of flack, "You are all a bunch of lesbians." One of the easiest, most powerful ways to put down a woman is for her sexuality.

The women's movement and certainly feminist family therapy are complicated, multifaceted movements. I don't think feminist family therapy is really one thing or ever will be. It's more a matter of perspective, how one thinks about the importance of gender in the therapy room. And the women's movement adds multiple dimensions of parts, and groups, and subgroups, and we are trying to talk to one another. We understand that sexism offends and is a reality, and we ought to be able to acknowledge the heterosexism and the power in that.

KM: Do you have any ideas about how we can continue to keep the work of feminist family therapists progressing and yet affirm White males and decrease their defensive reactions?

CR: (Laughter) How much time do we have? White men need to understand what's in it for them and what's in store for them if they don't change. Now, on a clinical level, the way I try to help my male clients (and my clientele is mostly White) is to help them look at what it's costing them to hold on to privilege, and hold on so tenaciously. In some cases, it is privileges about the money. "I earn the money, so I'm gonna decide whether we do this or that." In some cases, it is about how accountable they feel. Do they show up? Do they participate in family life? I don't believe that therapy is a vehicle in which it is useful or advisable to shame people, or to admonish them, or exhort them the way I might in a more appropriate setting. So I'm more inclined to try to help people see that it's in their own self-interests to relate to their partners in a respectful, egalitarian way, which I deeply believe is true.

I think that women who are treated respectfully and believe their husbands value their participation, their skills, and their contributions to family life are happier people. And they make happier wives, and their husbands are happier with them. I can't pretend that I'm not asking husbands to give up privilege, and I am just real direct about that.

I'd like a "wife" too. If I could do it without oppressing anybody, it would be great. Who wouldn't want somebody who carries me around in her head, and thinks about what do I need when she goes to Marshall Fields, or whether we really ought to schedule one more thing next week because I might have a tough week at the office, who protects me from people I don't want to deal with by interceding on the phone, who explains me to my children, or explains my children to me. Who wouldn't want such a thing? But unless that role, the role of whoever does that for you, is esteemed and elevated, then you end up with a person who feels badly abused. And people who feel badly abused generally do not make good roommates. They are not nice to live with, they're martyrs, or they are bitter, or they are angry all the time.

I try to talk to husbands about how it's in their self-interest to change, if that is what their wives are asking them to do. And of course, the women have to change too. There are so many contradictions for women now. The one that's the hardest for me, and the most gripping, is when a woman who's been begging her husband for years to open up, to be sensitive, to be vulnerable, and he does. Then she smacks him verbally, "I can't believe you're saying that," or "You should have thought about that 15 years ago," or "It feels unsexy, it feels too girlish, I don't want you all soft and vulnerable." That's very hard! You've got to be careful what you wish for.

I also think that women need to be challenged in those moments that this may bespeak the remnants of their own patriarchal thinking. Yes, they want to be equal, but they want him to be a little more equal. They want him to be the one to make the tough decisions, or to do the hard work, or to be strong and silent. Women need to work on those themselves, just as men need to work on their expectations. I think that there's hope, but I think it is a lot of hard work.

KM: My students frequently ask, "Why would any man come to see a feminist family therapist?" And then they argue about whether to call themselves feminist family therapists. They seem to get caught up in the idea that the man will be asked to give up privilege. And I say, "True, but if the couple or family was really happy and things were working, then they wouldn't be showing up for therapy."

CR: Right, right. I don't have any trouble asking anybody to give up privilege. The question about "What does it mean to call yourself a feminist therapist" is different. When somebody calls me up on the phone, I don't say, "By the way, did you know I'm a feminist therapist?" Because for one thing, I don't think a sexist therapist announces that he or she is sexist. It's not a category that the client is particularly interested in at that moment. When they come into the room, often they will ask, "How do you work?" "What is your theoretical orientation?" And then I say, "I am a feminist. I am interested in how gender informs couples' relationships and how gender constrains couples' relationships. My training also includes narrative, postmodern approaches," which doesn't mean much to anybody anyway. Basically I try to tell them, "Look, I try to listen very carefully to what you are telling me is the problem. And then I try to help you figure out how thinking about the problem differently would allow the problem to dissipate or be experienced differently." When I am working with couples, I show them that gender is one of the things that they are struggling with, and it is one of the things I know how to think about differently because I have been a feminist family therapist for a very long time. Actually, I have virtually no history of having difficulty with male clients. Male clients in my practice have appreciated my being direct about gender and privilege. In some sense, I think they identify with me because I am a very cognitively oriented person. I am very rationale and direct. I'm authoritative and don't mind saying, "Wait a second, you are interrupting, hold that thought." I direct things that need to be directed. It has just not come up. I've never had a man say, "Oh, you're a feminist? Ugh." Now it's not politically correct to do that anyway nowadays, so he just might not come back. But I also cannot say I have been aware of that. I don't think that they go away.

KM: It sometimes seems that viewing the world and the family in a patriarchal way is equated with neutrality and incorporating a feminist perspective or a feminist lens means you are biased, suggestive, and evaluative.

CR: I hope that we are getting beyond that. I thought we put to rest the notion that anyone is ever really neutral a while back. That was the big debate in the eighties when I "came out" as a feminist in the field. It was like, "That is so unneutral, that is such a bad thing," as if one can ever be neutral about gender. The evidence is overwhelming—you are not neutral about gender; you are gender. You either believe in supporting the status quo around gender or you don't. If you are supporting the status quo, that doesn't mean you are neutral—that means you are supporting the patriarchy. If you are not going to support patriarchy, then you are going to be feminist. I don't care what you call yourself.

My philosophy is, "If a man wants a green suit, put in a green light bulb." I am not so interested in labels. I'm very interested in descriptions. I think you can go further than labels and elaborate, "What are you trying to get at there?" "What does it mean to you to call yourself neutral, or gender sensitive, or feminist?" Then I can work with you on unpacking what might be problematic to me about that and how it might be problematic to you. I will get it out there in the open and talk about it. That is, in my mind, a feminist process.

KM: I recently heard a keynote address by Samuel Betances. He was very dynamic, and I liked a lot of his ideas. But the part that I struggled with was that he believed that, in order for us to continue to make progress, we had to actually be able to tell White men in particular that we appreciate them. We want to thank them for the generations of putting our systems in place. But that now with all the changing demographics, we have to do it all together, as partners.

CR: I don't really much care for appreciating a person as a member of a class—appreciating you as a White woman and for the sacrifices White women have made for generations. I could appreciate you as a person for what you have done or who you've been in my life. As a therapist, I could encourage your spouse or your children to appreciate that about you. I think that White men in my practice certainly develop an appreciation for the sacrifices they've made. They deserve empathy for the losses they've had—the loss of self, the loss of contact with their emotional needs. But I don't go for "You and the founding fathers are who got us to where we are," particularly in the clinical situation. I want to stay more in the here and now and talk about what you contribute to my life, or your wife's life, how the way that you are and how you behave toward your wife makes it difficult. I'd rather talk about that. Maybe on some social discourse or some political arena, it's useful to think about . . .

KM: And he is a sociologist so . . .

CR: In a clinical situation, I can't imagine doing that because it dilutes the concerns. I can't do anything about past generations. It dilutes a sense of personal efficacy and accountability, right now, right in the room. "What are you doing right now, for good or bad, in this system that needs to be addressed?"

KM: Another thing that I've heard more than once is that the effect that feminism had on family therapy was primarily in the 1970s and 1980s, and it is over with. Do you think that's true? Or what do you think are the most enduring or valuable . . .

CR: I absolutely don't think that's true. I think that the impact of the radicalness of the idea was in the 1970s and the 1980s. Now I think what's really exciting is the number of articles that are appearing in the journals that are very, very detailed analyses of exactly how husbands and wives, particularly in the marital therapy research, interrelate with each other around gender, how they use power, and how gender impacts conflict. That's very exciting to me; that's very exciting work.

I think we are past the level of critique—the critique is well established. We have offered up a broad view of how gender can be included in therapy, and this is being done differently by different therapists who have different models. We are researching real gender differences between men and women, which is going to then come back and inform therapy. That's not nearly as glamorous as Virginia Goldner writing this breathtakingly brilliant, intellectual piece about how gender has affected family therapy in its ideologies and its practices and then looking at how men and women make power moves differently in conflict (Goldner, 1985). Those are very different levels of impact on the field.

I think it's appropriate at this point that the emphasis is not on critique. We don't need more critique really. Unless of course, something stupid happens, and then I'll stand up and say, "Wait a second." (Laughter) We have a broad vision. Now the question is how to actualize it. What we need to know about is how men and women relate, how that manner of relating is held in place by gender beliefs, and how can we change those for people. That's where I think it is. I don't think that it's over. A lot of times when people say, "Oh, it's over now," that's wish fulfillment, that's what that is. "Please, please let it be over, please let us stop talking about this. I'm so tired of this." It is usually people of privilege, or people who are being asked to change, whether they are White, or they are male, or they are of European ancestry, whatever. Those are the people who will say, "Oh yeah, that was a really good thing, but now it's over. We are done with that, now we can move on to the next thing."

KM: You sound hopeful. Do you think most therapists that are in practice today inform couples and families about the connection of their problems to gender and power?

CR: No. (Laughter) I am hopeful, but I don't believe that is the case. I believe the leadership of the field has a significant sensitivity because those articles are appearing in the journals all the time, but then I think the daily practices of family therapists are still filled with unintended sexism. I think it's going to be a while before marriage isn't filled with unintended sexism. It is going to be a while.

KM: Our training . . .

CR: I think people who have a minimal understanding of gender process do much of our training.

KM: I think in some ways you've already addressed this point. But you do feel that women are hearing each other?

CR: Women are hearing each other? I'm sure they are. I know that there are some women, because I occasionally see them in treatment, who feel extremely isolated and marginalized. They believe that the problems that they are having are absolutely, 100% their problems and they have caused them. But I think that mostly, yes, women are hearing each other, and they have many different voices in which to hear.

Now I'm not talking about therapy, I'm talking about being on Oprah. There is a conversation going on in our culture that continually names the oppression that women have experienced. There are a large number of female comedians who talk about gender differences, often from a dry or bitter comedy perspective. Then there are women in film and other parts of the media who are strong and speak out on what they believe. There are women in politics. There's a whole broad conversation about gender that you almost can't help but hear. You may not agree with it or try to belittle it, but it's there, and it has not been going away. It has been getting louder and broader in many ways.

Whether or not a woman calls herself a feminist, and I don't want to play with semantics, but I think it's fewer than 10% of woman who would self-name themselves as feminists, the ideas that are being espoused by the majority of women in this country are feminist ideas. I think it's a conversation that can't be suppressed at this point.

KM: In your writings you have referred to therapy as a moral endeavor—one based on a vision of human life—and have stressed that moral questions should not be obscured. Can you comment further?

CR: I do believe that as much or more now than I did 10 years ago. I think that psychotherapy is a very, very specialized conversation that takes place in one of the few forums where people expect that their point of view will be deeply and respectfully received. They are safe to have known much of who they are. I think that inevitably must include their issues that touch on morality and moral character. It is not that therapy is primarily about people's moral character but exchanges about what's fair, what's due, what's owed, what's right—those are all charged with moral inferences. It's not like you can determine what's right in human relationships apart from some moral structure, whether it's religious, or humanitarian, or feminist, or something else. You've got to have some guidelines to help you know if it's OK that they are doing this stuff.

I think that is especially important when the clients are not even calling it into question. They have so internalized the oppression or the self-loathing that they are not even questioning that it might not be OK for their 13-year-old son to call his mother a bitch and a whore because he's mad at her. "He is just being an acting-out adolescent" hurts my feelings terribly. It's also a political statement because he wouldn't call his father that. Even if he were a very angry, acting-out adolescent, he wouldn't call his father things that have reference to his father's sexuality. That's a gender-based kind of accusation. It comes out of a refusal to comply with one moral code and the imposition of another. It says something like, "I get to call you whatever I want and hurt you anyway I can. I can use things that I know are going to get you more 'cause you are a woman and I am a male saying it to you." I would want to challenge that, and one of the grounds that I would challenge it on is moral.

It is not a moral way of treating human beings to belittle them on the basis of being a member of some category. It makes them less than fully human.

KM: In light of all the changes in our families and society, what are your ideas about what needs to happen in our larger society?

CR: From sexual liberation to equality between genders—it has to do with families and the children. We have not solved the problem of who is going to raise the children. Whether it's through on-site child care, more parental leave, or fathers taking as much responsibility as mothers, which would radicalize the workforce, something has to happen. Because right now, we are still left with women participating in higher numbers than ever in the workforce and still feeling a vast majority of burden around child care. That's not a situation that lends itself to equality. Furthermore, it lends for a lot of exhausted women, angry women, and frustrated husbands whose wives are always tired.

A lot of kids fall between the cracks because parents just aren't giving them as much as they need. There are not good alternatives for most kids. The number of really excellent daycare facilities in most areas is very small, and it looks like that's not very good care for babies. Babies need to be with their parents or a parentlike figure, and most of us can't afford that.

How are we going to take care of the babies and the children in a way that doesn't land the entire burden on the backs of women? If we cannot do that, not just women's liberation but family life itself is going to be very constrained. It's very difficult. That's where I see the big work that needs to be done. There are things we need to change in our institutions and our political process. Not so much the political structure but the political process.

The big thing is, so far, in relationship to family, the people who control work environments, the owners of industry, have really not put a lot of energy in it. I don't think it's going to happen until the fathers say, "I'm a highly skilled worker and I am just not going to put up with this and you can't replace me very easily." The women doing it is not enough; it's got to be the men too. When they do it, then it will happen.

It is not that it cannot be done; it has been done in other societies. We just haven't made it a priority here. I don't think it is going to be until men are willing to risk whatever negatives come to them for saying, "I am a father and I want to be responsible for my children. I can't be working under the constrictions and restrictions now in place."

KM: Do you think we are any closer to that?

CR: I don't know overall. I don't track labor stuff very closely. I hear anecdotes that are encouraging. But in my practice, I hear these very difficult, second-shift kind of stories—women working until they drop.

KM: Any advice for our sons and daughters?

CR: Of course you have probably inferred that I think we should carefully raise all of our daughters to be feminist, as we should our sons. With my son, I really try to help him understand that whatever privileges accrue to him by being a man, if he exploits those it could cost him his partner, his marriage. It will be very costly; he will pay a lot for those privileges in terms of the satisfactions that he can draw from relationships.

One of the things that the literature is becoming clear about is men can be intimate with women who they feel equal to, not lower in status. If they feel unequal in the relationship, they don't want to be vulnerable. And I think intimacy is a great thing. We almost all need intimacy, long for it, or we defend against it. We all had disappointing experiences and deceive ourselves about it. I don't think we can expect to have intimacy if we don't have equality in the relationship. I think it's in the self-interest of men to pursue equality.

KM: I know we have covered a lot of territory. Is there anything that you would like to add in terms of the context of your life?

CR: I guess it's already been implied, but let me just say, I don't consider myself sitting up at the top of any mountain looking down on anyone telling them how it should be. Like everybody else who has worked down in the trenches, I am embedded in a life that is gendered and I cannot get away from that. I am both holding myself accountable to try to be clear headed about gender constraints, and moving beyond them, as I am trying to help my clients hold themselves accountable for the very same thing. It's very much a participatory process for me. Even though in the 50 minutes I may be in the consulting room with clients, I am trying to offer a position of some expertise to them, at the same time, I know I don't have it all figured out and I'm not setting myself apart from it all.

KM: This really was just an absolute thrill for me. Thank you.

References

Chesler, P. (1972). *Women and madness.* Garden City, NY: Doubleday.
Gilligan, C. (1982). *In a different voice.* Cambridge, MA: Harvard University Press.

Goldner, V. (1985). Feminism and family therapy. *Family Process, 24*, 31–47.

Goodrich, T. J., Rampage, C., Ellman, B., & Halstead, K. (1988). *Feminist family therapy: A casebook.* New York: Norton.

Hare-Mustin, R. (1978). A feminist approach to family therapy. *Family Process, 17*, 181–194.

Hare-Mustin, R. (1987). The problem of gender in family therapy. *Family Process, 26*, 15–28.

Real, T. (1998). *I don't want to talk about it: Overcoming the legacy of male depression.* New York: Fireside.

Walters, M., Carter, B., Papp, P., & Silverstein, O. (1988). *The invisible web: Gender patterns in family relationships.* New York: Gulford Press.

■ ■ ■